Paul Shorey

Pope's the Iliad of Homer

Books I, VI, XXII, and XXIV. Vol. 1

Paul Shorey

Pope's the Iliad of Homer
Books I, VI, XXII, and XXIV. Vol. 1

ISBN/EAN: 9783337240387

Printed in Europe, USA, Canada, Australia, Japan

Cover: Foto ©Thomas Meinert / pixelio.de

More available books at **www.hansebooks.com**

Heath's English Classics

POPE'S

THE ILIAD OF HOMER

BOOKS I, VI, XXII, AND XXIV

EDITED WITH AN INTRODUCTION AND NOTES

BY

PAUL SHOREY, Ph.D.

PROFESSOR IN THE UNIVERSITY OF CHICAGO

BOSTON, U.S.A.

D. C. HEATH & CO., PUBLISHERS

1899

CONTENTS.

iii

INTRODUCTION.

HOMER AND THE ILIAD.

GREEK literature begins with the *Iliad*, a masterpiece which remained for a thousand years the Bible and the Milton of the nation. Such a poem presupposes a long process of growth. No one bard invented the chief personages and incidents of the tale of Troy, or shaped the Homeric hexameter into "the stateliest measure ever moulded by the lips of man." But for the history of this development we are reduced to mere conjecture. There may have been a long line of ballad poets preceding Homer, as well as of epic poets contemporary with or succeeding him. The *Iliad*, as we have it, is certainly not the work of one literary artist in the sense in which this may be said of Virgil's *Æneid* or of Milton's *Paradise Lost*. Yet its unity of design and style convince competent judges of poetry that it was shaped in the main by one transcendent genius, whether we conceive him preferably as the inventor of a framework filled out by others or as the poet who harmonized and supplemented a loose collection of pre-existing lays.

Only a little less vague is our knowledge of the precise relation of this unknown Homer to the beginnings and prehistoric origins of Greek civilization. The *Iliad* describes an expedition of the chieftains of Argos, Sparta, and Mycenæ, and other towns of European Greece, against a city in northwestern Asia Minor. On the traditional site of Troy Schliemann has discovered the remains of a prehistoric city answering fairly well to Homer's descriptions.[1] At Mycenæ, the traditional seat of Agamemnon's power, and at the neighboring Tiryns, the spade of the archæologist has uncovered tombs, citadels, and rock-built palaces that fit our conceptions of the palaces and the graves of the great Homeric monarchs. Greek history tells us of the overthrow of an earlier civilization in the Peloponnesus by rude Dorian tribes from the north who expelled the older dynasties and founded the historic states of Argos, Sparta, and Mycenæ. An extensive emigration to Asia Minor was brought about by this shifting of populations, and the Greek cities of Asia Minor thus founded or renewed were the seat of the first efflorescence of Greek commerce, letters, and philosophy.[2]

These few facts have been worked up by scholars into every conceivable permutation and combination. One of the most plausible of these theories is that, while the outline of the *Iliad* was composed in continental Greece in honor of the Thessalian hero Achilles, the poem, as we have it, is a product of the Greek civilization of Asia Minor. The poet or poets who sang to the princes and rich burghers of the Asiatic Greek cities created in the story of the siege of Troy an ideal picture of the long series of obscure conflicts by which their ancestors established themselves upon the coast of Asia.

With regard to these and similar problems we may say to the young student of Homer as literature what Matthew Arnold says to the translator of Homer: "These are questions which have been discussed with learning, with ingenuity, nay, with genius; but they have two inconveniences, —

[1] Cf. Schuchhardt's Schliemann (Eng. translation). Holm, *History of Greece* (translation), Vol. I, p. 76.

[2] Holm, Vol. I, chap. xii, p. 135.

one general for all who approach them, one particular for the translator. The general inconvenience is that there really exist no data for determining them. The particular inconvenience is that their solution by the translator, even were it possible, could be of no benefit to his translation."

Regarded merely as a story the *Iliad* is a short episode in the siege of Troy, one of the four great tales of Grecian legend. Homer, as Horace observes in the *Ars Poetica*, does not begin the Trojan war with an account of the swan's egg, from which Helen was born, but plunges boldly into the midst of things and sweeps his hearer on with only occasional allusions to the rest of the story as we find it systematically set forth in the hand-books of mythology.

That story, as a whole, was known to the Greeks from other epic poems of which only a few lines of fragments remain. These, the so-called Cyclic poems or epics of the cycle, were sometimes attributed to Homer by the uncritical, but were later than the *Iliad*. They seem to have been arranged in a continuous series leading up to and supplementing the *Iliad* and *Odyssey*. A sufficient account of the little that is known about them will be found in Jebb's *Introduction to Homer*, p. 153, and in Lang's *Homer and the Epic*, p. 322 sqq. From these lost epics were derived many of the episodes with which the Greek dramatists and later poets embellished the legend.

The story as thus known is charmingly told, with some sentimental modern touches, by Andrew Lang in his pretty poem, *Helen of Troy*. In Lang's version the *Iliad* proper is represented only by stanzas xi–xxi of Book V. All that precedes is the "things before Homer" and what follows the "things after Homer".—the latter known to us now mainly from the account of the capture of Troy in the second book of Virgil's *Æneid*, and from the *Post-Homerica* of Quintus of Smyrna, an epic poet of the fourth century A.D.

The tale of Troy is in outline this: Zeus and Poseidon loved Thetis, daughter of the old man of the sea, but relinquished her to King Peleus of Thessaly because of a prophecy that she was to bear a son mightier than his sire. Zeus, desirous to relieve the earth of the burden of over-population, made the marriage of Peleus and Thetis the occasion of a great war. "When all the full-faced presence of the gods ranged in the halls of Peleus,"[1] Discord, alone not invited, cast upon the board a golden apple whose gleaming rind was engraven "For the most fair." The prize was claimed by Hera, Athena, and Aphrodite, and the arbitrament was referred to Paris, a son of King Priam of Troy, who had been exposed as a babe upon Mount Ida and brought up by shepherds in ignorance of his rank because of the ill-boding dream of his mother Hecuba and the dire omens that attended his birth. The " Judgment of Paris " is a favorite theme of later poetry and painting, and is known to English readers from the poems of Parnell and Beattie, and Tennyson's beautiful *Œnone*. Homer alludes to it but once and briefly in the words: "But they (Hera and Athena) continued as when at the beginning sacred Ilios became hateful to them, and Priam and his people, by reason of the sin of Alexandros (Paris) in that he contemned those goddesses when they came to his steading, and preferred her who brought him deadly lustfulness." By 'her who brought him deadly lustfulness' is meant Aphrodite, who promised him "the fairest and most loving wife in Greece."

By the help of Aphrodite Paris obtained recognition of his birth, built a fleet of ships and sailed across seas to the court of Menelāus, king of Sparta, where he won the love of Helen the wife of Menelaus, and bore her back to Troy, together with much stolen treasure.

Helen, nominally the daughter of Tyndarĕus, was, accord-

---

[1] Tennyson's *Œnone*.

ing to later legend, really the child of Zeus. All the princes
of Greece sought her in marriage, and all, in the post-Homeric
story, swore to defend the rights of the man whom her father
should select. Menelaus accordingly summoned his brother
Agamemnon, the great king of Mycenæ rich in gold, and
other prominent chieftains, to help him to recover Helen and
revenge the wrong done to Greece.

Ten years were spent in collecting a mighty host with the
aid of Hera and Athena. Embassies were sent to demand
redress in vain. At last a fleet of 1186 ships and 100,000
men was assembled at Aulis in Eubœa under the command
of Agamemnon.

The second book of the *Iliad* contains a catalogue of this
force, a sort of Domesday Book of early Greece. The most
prominent leaders under Agamemnon and Menelaus were
wise old Nestor of Pylos, with 90 ships, Idomeneus of Crete
and Diomede of Argos, with 80 each, Achilles, son of Peleus,
and his bosom friend Patroclus, from Phthia and Hellas, with
50 ships, Ajax Telamon from Salamis with 12, and Odysseus
of Ithaca with 12.

The Trojans, of whom a list is also given, were outnum-
bered by the Greeks in the proportion of ten to one. Their
bravest leaders were Hector, son of Priam, his cousin Æneas,
best known as the hero of the Æneid, and the leaders of the
Lycian allies, Glaucus and Sarpēdon.

At this point later legend introduces two stories ignored by
Homer. One relates how the Greeks, missing their bearings,
landed on the coast of Mysia and after various adventures
returned to Greece for a fresh start. The other is the pathetic
legend of the sacrifice of Agamemnon's daughter Iphigenīa
to propitiate the wrath of Artemis who was detaining the
fleet at Aulis by adverse winds — a favorite theme of later
poetry known to English readers from the exquisite verses
of Landor and the four beautiful stanzas in Tennyson's

Dream of Fair Women. Another pathetic incident marked the arrival of the Greeks at Troy. An oracle had declared that the first Greek to set foot on Trojan soil must fall. When all others shrank back Protesilāus, though he had left a young bride and an unfinished home behind, offered himself a willing victim. The story, just glanced at in a line of the catalogue of ships, is the theme of Wordsworth's *Laodameia.*

The incidents invented by later legend to fill the nine years of siege that precede the *Iliad* need not detain us. The Greeks are conceived as encamped in huts built about the sterns of their ships drawn up on the Trojan strand. They were unable to invest the city and were obliged to supply their wants by forays into the surrounding country and attacks on neighboring towns and islands. Glimpses of these expeditions are afforded by Achilles's boasts of the number of cities he has taken by sea and land.

So long as Achilles kept the field the Trojans rarely ventured to descend to open combat in the plain between Troy and the ships. In the tenth year Achilles's quarrel with Agamemnon about the beautiful captives, Chryseïs and Briseïs, gave them a respite until Hector slew Patroclus, and love for his dead friend triumphing over every other passion in Achilles's breast hurled him into the war again, there to slay Hector, the chief support of Troy. This episode is the *Iliad.* The action of the poem occupies about 45 days, of which the first book takes 21. The 22d day extends through the sixth book to line 380 of the seventh. Hector is slain in Book XXII on the 27th day.

The following summary of the plot is slightly abbreviated from that given in Jebb's *Homer,* p. 6: —

I. In the tenth year of the war, Apollo plagues the Greeks, because the daughter of Chryses, his priest, has been taken by Agamemnon, who, being required to restore her, wrongs Achilles by depriving him

of his captive, the maiden Briseis. Thereupon Achilles retires from
the war, and Zeus swears to Thetis, the hero's mother, that the Greeks
shall rue this wrong done to her son.

II. Agamemnon's beguiling dream. Marshalling of the army.
Catalogue of Greek and Trojan forces.

III. Duel between Paris and Menelaus. Helen and Priam view the
Greek hosts from the walls of Troy. Aphrodite saves Paris.

IV. The Trojan Pandarus breaks the truce. Agamemnon marshals
the Greeks. The armies join battle.

V. Exploits of Diomede, who, helped by Athena, wounds Aphrodite
and Ares.

VI. Interview of Diomede and the Lycian Glaucus on the field of
battle. Hector, returning to Troy, bids farewell to Andromache before
going out to battle again.

VII. Duel of Hector and Ajax. Burying of the dead. The Greeks
build a wall to protect their camp.

VIII. Fighting, interrupted at 485 by the gods. At night the Trojans
bivouac on the field. Famous moonlight scene. ·

IX. Agamemnon sends envoys to Achilles by night, offering amends
and the restoration of Briseis. Achilles spurns the offer in a magnificent speech.

X. Episode of the night expedition of Odysseus and Diomede, who
slay the spy Dolon and the sleeping Rhesus, chief of the Thracians.

XI. Great deeds of Agamemnon, who is finally disabled with many
others. Patroclus, sent by Achilles, learns that the plight of the Greeks
is desperate.

XII. The Trojans, led by Hector, break through the wall of the
Greek camp.

XIII. Zeus, having turned his eyes away, Poseidon encourages the
Greeks.

XIV. The sleep god and Hera lull Zeus to sleep on Ida. Poseidon
urges on the Greeks, and Hector is wounded.

XV. Zeus awakens. At his bidding Apollo restores Hector. The
Trojans attack the ships, which Ajax bravely defends.

XVI. Patroclus intercedes for the Greeks with Achilles who lends
him his armor. In the guise of his friend, Patroclus leads the Myrmidons to battle, drives back the Trojans, and at last is slain by Hector.

XVII. Fight over the corpse of Patroclus.

XVIII. Achilles learns the death of Patroclus, and makes moan for
him; at the sound whereof, Thetis rises from the sea, and comes to her

son. She persuades the god of fire, Hephæstus, to make new armor
for Achilles. The shield wrought by Hephæstus is described.

XIX. Reconciliation of Agamemnon and Achilles. Restoration of
Briseis. Achilles goes forth to battle. The horse Xanthus speaks with
a human voice and foretells the doom of Achilles.

XX. The gods come down to join in the battle. Achilles fights with
Æneas, who is saved by Poseidon; and with Hector, who is saved by
Apollo.

XXI. The river god Scamander fights with Achilles, who is saved
by Hephæstus.

XXII. Achilles fights with Hector, and chases him thrice round the
walls of Troy. Zeus weighs in golden scales the lots of Achilles and
Hector. Hector is doomed to die; Apollo deserts him, while Athena
lures him to his doom and aids Achilles. Achilles slays Hector.
Lament of Andromache.

XXIII. The spirit of Patroclus appears to Achilles and craves burial.
The funeral rites and games.

XXIV. As Achilles daily drags the corpse of Hector round the
barrow of Patroclus, Apollo pleads with the gods, and Zeus stirs up
Priam to go and ransom the body of his son. The god Hermes, in
disguise, conducts the aged king across the plain; Achilles receives
him courteously, and accepts the ransom; and Priam goes back to
Troy with the corpse of Hector, to be mourned and buried.

The *Iliad* is no garrulous chronicle of a ten years' war. It
is not a history or a biography. Its subject is not Achilles,
but the wrath of Achilles. For, as Aristotle says in his *Poetics*, many things happen to one man that are connected by
no inner or rational bond, and it is therefore an æsthetic error
to choose such a subject for a poem as *The Life and Death
of Jason*. The unity of the *Iliad* is spiritual and dramatic.
It is the portrayal of a mighty conflict of passions in a great
and noble but erring soul, and the effects of that conflict on
the destinies of two contending armies, and of many brave
men and beautiful women.

Dante sums it up in a line when he speaks of "great
Achilles who at the last was brought to fight by love." And
Ruskin in *Sesame and Lilies* expands the same thought in

his eloquent way: "The main features in the character of Achilles are its intense desire of justice and its tenderness of affection. And in that bitter song of the *Iliad*, this man, though aided continually by the wisest of the gods and burning with the desire of justice in his heart, becomes yet, through ill-governed passion, the most unjust of men; and, full of the deepest tenderness in his heart, becomes yet, through ill-governed passion, the most cruel of men. Intense alike in love and friendship, he loses first his mistress, and then his friend; for the sake of the one he surrenders to death the armies of his own land ; for the sake of the other he surrenders all. Will a man lay down his life for his friend? Yea — even for his *dead* friend, this Achilles, though goddess-born, and goddess-taught, gives up his kingdom, his country, and his life — casts alike the innocent and guilty, with himself, into one gulf of slaughter, and dies at last by the hand of the basest of his adversaries."

It is possible to select from the twenty-four books of the *Iliad* a "Story of Achilles" that shall move more swiftly and directly to the goal of Achilles's reappearance in the field to avenge upon Hector the death of Patroclus. But we must not infer that such a skeleton plot is æsthetically better or historically nearer to the original design than the *Iliad* as we have it.[1]

A significant dramatic episode makes a better epic than a long-drawn chronicle. But the episode will interest us little unless it is so narrated as to bring before our minds the larger action of which it is a part. It is only by an unreal abstraction of scholars that the story of Achilles or Achilleïd can be conceived apart from the song of Ilium or the Iliad. The twenty-second book is the climax of the *Iliad*. It is there that the pity and terror culminate when Hector makes his last stand without the walls which he has defended so long,

[1] Jebb's fourth chapter contains as much of the erudition of the Homeric question as the young student can possibly use.

and around which he has thrice fled in an access of irresistible terror before the embittered foe who is now to slay him. But how should this combat move us more than any other encounter of clamorous spear-brandishing warriors of the age of bronze if we did not know the sacred Ilium from which Priam and Hecuba look down in unavailing anguish? What would Andromache be to us that we should weep for her when she falls fainting on the great tower of Ilium to see that gracious head trailed in the dust in his enemy's day if we had not in our minds that other picture of Hector's babe clinging to the nurse's bosom scared at the father's glittering crest while the mother stands by smiling through her tears? What tragic lesson should we read in Achilles's wrath if we were simply told that he cherished his grudge against the Greeks for suffering Agamemnon to rob him of Briseis until it was banished from his mind by the fiercer passion of his thirst for revenge upon Hector? We must witness the consequences of that wrath in the books where Achilles is conspicuous by his absence. We must observe the failure of the heroism of Diomede and Ajax, and of the sagacious policy of Odysseus and Nestor to supply his place. We must have seen him, in the ninth book, relentlessly spurn the atonement proffered by Agamemnon and the humbled mediation of the noblest Greeks, his friends. We must have watched his passion exalt itself to the height of the pride and ruthlessness that invite the cruel nemesis which overtakes him in the end. Then, when fire has been hurled upon the Grecian ships, and Patroclus has been slain, and Achilles clad in the divine armor at last goes forth to seek " him who has laid low so dear a head," we understand the whirlwind of conflicting passions, shame, remorse, grief, fierce thirst for revenge and foreboding of his own untimely death that sweep him on; we can comprehend, if not pardon, his cruelty, and can admit that even Hector, brave though he be, may well shrink before that " terror of the plain."

But all this means that the climax of the poem æsthetically justifies if it does not absolutely guaranty the main structure of our *Iliad*. We must have the second and third books to acquaint us with Troy town and introduce the chief *dramatis personæ*. Without the sixth book Hector, Andromache, Paris, and Helen are mere names. The ninth book is required for the development of the character of Achilles and the justification of the nemesis that falls upon him. After this let us concede that interpolators may be responsible for repetitions and unnecessary scenes in Books II–VIII, and for the confusion and drawing out of the fighting in Books XI–XVII; that the fifth and tenth books may be treated as detachable episodes, and the twenty-third and twenty-fourth as afterpieces. We can neither prove nor disprove it, and it does not matter.

The least attractive feature of the *Iliad* to the modern reader is the interminable slashing and foining and spear-hurling of the battle scenes. This feeling is brutally expressed by Roscommon in his *Essay on Translated Verse:* —

> " For who, without a qualm, hath ever looked
> On holy garbage though by Homer cooked?
> Whose railing heroes and whose wounded gods
> Make some suspect he snores as well as nods."

For the discerning student of the original, this monotony of butchery is redeemed by the splendid fiery energy that informs the best battle pieces, and by relieving touches of grim irony or exquisite pathos that escape the careless reader. But an explicit defence of Homer on this score is not required here, since the books selected for this volume contain little fighting.

*   *   *   *   *   *   *   *   *   *

A source of interest in Homer which we must be careful neither to overrate nor underestimate is the light he throws on the life, institutions, and feelings of early man. The forty-eight books of the *Iliad* and *Odyssey* contain materials for an almost complete reconstruction of the life of the Homeric man: his conception of the universe; his knowledge of Mediterranean geography; the animals, plants, metals, tools, and industrial processes with which he was acquainted; his house, his family, his eating, his dress, his arms and armor, his government in peace and war, his religion and mythology, his elementary, but generally wholesome, notions of conduct and life. This material has been systematically collected in three enormous volumes,[1] which, as the perhaps apocryphal German professor said, will spare you the trouble of reading the poems themselves. A brief, but quite sufficient account of "Homer's world" will be found in the second chapter of Jebb's *Introduction to Homer*, to which occasional reference is made in the notes. To summarize the summary here would serve no useful end.

While recognizing this side of Homer, we must yet remember that we are concerned with the *Iliad* as a masterpiece of literature. And, regarded as a great poem in the "grand style," the *Iliad*, in spite of its naïvetés and "survivals," is more nearly akin to the other masterpieces of the world's literature than it is to the ballads and popular epics to which it is so often likened. For some purposes of scholars the *Iliad* may be instructively compared with the collection of Finnish legends known as the *Kalevala*, with the mediæval French *Chanson de Roland*, or the Teutonic *Edda* and *Niebelungen Lied*. But it is fundamentally discriminated from all "popular epics" by the fact that, like the *Æneid* and *Paradise Lost*, it ranks among the few supremely great and beautiful creations of the artistic genius of man — and they do not. The student then will make a mistake if, in watching for the primitive or savage notes in the *Iliad*, he misses the essential grace, dignity, and elevation of its manner and

[1] Buchholz, *Homerische Realien.*

outlook upon life. Whatever the *Iliad* may be as a "document," it is primarily for us a thrilling tale of noble, though simple, types of men and women told in magnificent verse. When Mr. Goldwin Smith, in his discussion of Cowper's translation, permits himself to speak of "Hector's Andromache" as "the savage woman," he commits a grosser error in criticism than can be found in the most periwigged, high-heeled, and powdered paraphrase of Pope.

* * * * * * * * * *

A volume might easily be made of the praises of Homer. "My father, anxious that I should become a good man, made me learn all the poems of Homer," says the young man in Xenophon's *Banquet*. "The eulogists of Homer declare (says Plato) that he has been the educator of Hellas, and that he is profitable for education and for the ordering of human things, and that you should take him up again and again, and get to know him, and regulate your whole life according to him."

Æschylus said that his tragedies were scraps from the banquet of Homer, and indeed all Greek literature might be studied as a development or expansion of the *Iliad* and *Odyssey*. "Homer," says an eloquent moral philosopher of the first century, "is the beginning, the middle, and the end, to every child, youth, and old man, imparting so much as each is able to accept."

Latin literature began with a translation of Homer, which long remained the first schoolbook of Roman youth. Quintilian, in his treatise on the *Education of an Orator*, says, "As Aratus declares, we must begin with Jove, so we affirm that the true beginning is with Homer, from whom as from his own ocean all lesser streams and rivulets are derived." "All Greek gentlemen," says Ruskin, "were educated on Homer, all Roman gentlemen on Greek literature, all modern gentlemen on Greek and Roman literature." Victor Hugo cries out in

his intense way : " Of all the books that are in the hands of
men, two only must be studied by the poet — Homer and the
Bible ; " and the critical Matthew Arnold deliberately affirms
that " whatever may be the fate of classical study in general,
attention will be more and more directed to the poetry of
Homer, not indeed as part of a classical course, but as the
most important poetical monument existing " Sayings like
these, which might be multiplied indefinitely, testify to the im-
mense hold of Homer upon the minds of men, to his infinite
charm.   The nature and cause of that charm are not easy to
define.

> " Sweet, tell me what is Homer's sting,
> Old Homer's sting," she said :
> " He stirs my sluggish pulse like wine,
> He melts me like the wind of spice,
> Strong as strong Ajax' red right hand,
> And grand like Juno's eyes."

The potency of this spell is not confined to those who can
enjoy the music of the original.   " A few days ago," said the
French sculptor, Bouchardon, " an old French book that I
never heard of fell into my hands.   It is called the *Iliad* of
Homer.   Since I read that book men are fifteen feet high to
me, and I cannot sleep."   Keats, too, knew the *Iliad* only in
Chapman's version when he thrilled

> " Like some watcher of the skies
> When a new planet swims into his ken ;
>   Or, like stout Cortez, when, with eagle eyes,
> He stared at the Pacific — and all his men
>   Looked at each other with a wild surmise—
> Silent upon a peak in Darien."

An appreciation of all the varied excellences that call forth
these enthusiastic laudations can come only with close study.
One chief cause of Homer's supreme fascination for the spirit

of modern man has been summed up in a sentence by Professor Jebb: "The union of consummate art in poetical form with the spiritual character of a simple age is the unique distinction of the Homeric poems." We live in a complicated indoor world of books, inherited traditions and institutions, the rationale of which we dimly apprehend, mechanical appliances that we use without understanding, social forms that disguise the play of natural feeling. It is our world. We should be content in no other. The aspirations of a Rousseau or a Thoreau for an impracticable life according to nature are mere rhetoric. And yet deep down below the surface the primitive instincts persist and thirst for satisfaction. We long for an outdoor life, for immediate contact with and direct manipulation of the material things and processes by which our daily life is sustained; for a franker and more naïve display of the feelings of the natural man; for a relief from the dead superincumbent load of custom, tradition, and accumulation of the written word. This relief we find in "picnics" and summer outings — more adventurous spirits in exploration, pioneering, and war. But we experience its charm vicariously in the literature of more primitive ages that lived habitually in the direct contact with the physical world denied to us, and in the recognition of the great underlying facts of existence which the conventions of modern life disguise. But generally our enjoyment of this order of literature is impaired by an inner dissidence arising from the shock it gives to our tastes and moral instincts. The expression is not only naïve, but grotesque and unbeautiful. The men and women are not only natural and unsophisticated, but brutal and animal — not of childlike but of childish mind, too remote for sympathy. In Homer, broadly speaking, this is not the case. He takes us back to what relatively to us is the childhood of the world. With him we fade far away and quite forget "the weariness, the fever, and the fret," of what in moods of yearning reaction toward nature we call the "strange disease of modern life." But escaping artificiality, we still dwell in the realm of an art whose never failing law is grace and beauty; and, while freed from conventionality and explicit moral didacticism, we are still in a world of instinctively noble men and women, whose natures we can understand and with whose joy and grief we can feel an unforced sympathy. And to this unique combination of primitive simplicity with moral nobility and æsthetic charm, the lovers of Homer pay the tribute of an admiration that seems idolatrous to those who have never known his spell.

II. POPE AND POPE'S ILIAD.

ALEXANDER POPE was born in London, May 22, 1688. His father was a Roman Catholic merchant who retired from business soon after the poet's birth, and established his home at Binfield in Windsor Forest. Owing to a sickly constitution and the disabilities that attached to his religion, Pope's education was irregular. He was a precocious lad "who lisped in numbers, for the numbers came." He early acquired a smattering of the Greek, Latin, French, and Italian languages, read widely if unsystematically in poetry and *belles lettres*, and made the acquaintance of the leading wits and literary men of the day. His first published work, the *Pastorals*, an artificial imitation of Virgil's *Eclogues*, appeared in 1709, but was composed three or four years earlier. The *Essay on Criticism* followed, a cleverly rhymed summary of the best things said by Boileau, Horace, and the ancient rhetoricians about literature, criticism, and style. In 1712 he published the first edition of the *Rape of the Lock*, a dainty, ingenious, mock-heroic epic dealing with the "wrath," not of Achilles, but of a society belle who resented the liberty taken by a noble young peer who had surreptitiously severed a lock of her hair. This was followed in 1713 by the pastoral poem, *Windsor Forest.* At twenty-five (Dryden having been dead thirteen years) Pope was admittedly the first poet of the age, and when he issued the prospectus of a translation of Homer to be published by subscription men of all parties hastened to subscribe to what was felt to be a great national work. In November, 1713, "Bishop Kennet saw Swift in all his glory, and wrote an often quoted description of the scene. Swift was bustling about in the royal antechamber, swelling with conscious importance, distributing advice, promising patronage, whispering to ministers, and filling the whole room with his presence. He finally 'instructed a young nobleman that the best poet in England was Mr. Pope, a Papist, who had begun a translation of Homer into English verse, for which he must have them all subscribe; "for," says he, "the author shall not begin to print till I have a thousand guineas for him!"'"[1]

The translation of Homer occupied Pope for ten or twelve years. The *Iliad* was completed in 1720, the *Odyssey*, of which his assistants, Fenton and Broome, did about half, in 1726. To this long labor Pope refers feelingly in a distich of the *Dunciad* (3. 331) : —

> "Hibernian politics, O Swift! thy fate;
> And Pope's, ten years to comment and translate."

He had his reward, however. Subscriptions and sales brought him in about £9000, an enormous sum for those days, and made him independent for life. In 1718 he established himself for the remainder of his days in the villa at Twickenham on Thames that has always been associated with his name and with the friendships of Arbuthnot, Gay, Bolingbroke, and Swift, who visited him there. His other chief

[1] Leslie Stephen, Pope, in *English Men of Letters.*

works are the *Dunciad*, 1728, a satire on his literary enemies, Theobald, Cibber, Dennis Lintot, and other subjects of the great goddess Dulness; the *Essay on Man*, 1732–1734, a brilliant epigrammatic versification of eighteenth-century rationalistic optimism and odds and ends of philosophy learned from Bolingbroke or picked up by desultory reading; the *Satires and Epistles of Horace Imitated*, 1733–1738; and *Moral Essays* (in verse), 1731–1735. He died on the 30th of May, 1744, and was buried at Twickenham.

His rank as a poet has been endlessly debated by critics. The question is one of definition. If we reserve the name of poetry for exquisite song, for "natural magic," or the "vision and the faculty divine," for things like Keats's odes, Shelley's lyrics, and Wordsworth's best sonnets, then Pope and Dryden were, as Matthew Arnold says, rather great prose writers in verse than great poets. If terse epigrammatic expression of unimpeachable good sense in smoothly rhymed verse suffices to make a poet, then few names in English literature stand higher than Pope's. His contribution to the dictionary of familiar quotations exceeds that of all but Shakspere.

The *Iliad* is perhaps his greatest achievement. Like Amyot's *Plutarch*, Fitzgerald's *Omar Khayyam*, and Jowett's *Plato*, it holds the place in literary history rather of an original masterpiece than of a translation. Modern taste demands that the translator of Homer shall endeavor to reproduce for us by conscious archaism something of the atmosphere of the world's childhood. Pope did not attempt that. Scholars who know the original will be provoked into repeating the words of Bentley: "It is a pretty poem, Mr. Pope, but you must not call it Homer." But regarded simply as a readable poem, reproducing the substance of the Homeric story in a style of sustained finish, vivacity, and point, it occupies a place which no other version can claim. Its merits were amply recognized. Johnson said that it had tuned the English tongue, and that it was the noblest version of poetry the world had ever seen. Gray declared that no other translation could ever equal it, and Gibbon said that it had every merit except that of fidelity to the original. Byron thought that no one would ever lay it down except for Homer himself. Endless is the tale of the poets and writers whose biographers affirm that their first literary inspiration was derived from its pages. It became the accepted model of poetic style for a century. Coleridge observes that it was the main source of that pseudo-poetic diction for which he and Wordsworth endeavored to substitute the unaffected language of the heart. Modern taste has now grown weary of this artificial diction in which "a woman is called a nymph — and women generally are 'the fair' — in which shepherds are conscious swains, and a poet invokes the muses, and strikes a lyre, and breathes on a reed."[1] But it has exercised an enormous influence on the style of those who repudiate it, and an observant reader could collect from Byron, Scott, nay, even from Wordsworth and Shelley, a long list of poetical tags, epithets, and paraphrases taken straight from the pages of Pope's *Iliad*.

Many attempts have been made to supersede it in popular favor, but for the majority of readers it still remains the one poetical translation of Homer. The early versions of Hobbes and Ogilby are of interest only to professional students of literature. Chapman is praised on the faith of Keats's noble sonnet, and because of occasional spirited passages and exquisite lines. It is true in a sense, as Lowell says, that he is the only translator who seems to be inspired by Homer. But the rugged rhythms, the obscurity of the syntax, the fantastic Elizabethan conceits, and the long uninspired tracts of doggerel that intervene between the fine quotable passages make him intolerable in continuous perusal. Cowper,

[1] Leslie Stephen.

in his blank verse version, aimed at uniting Miltonic stateliness with fidelity to Homeric simplicity, but succeeded only
in being pompous and dull. All these, together with the
quaintly exact version of Professor Newman, are interestingly
discussed in Matthew Arnold's classic lectures *On Translating
Homer*. There are four Homeric qualities which Arnold
thinks the translator must especially feel and strive to reproduce: (1) He is eminently rapid; (2) he is plain and
direct in his syntax and in his words; (3) he is plain and
direct in his matter and ideas; (4) he is noble in his
manner.

Since the publication of Matthew Arnold's essay we have
had, among others, the estimable blank verse translations of
Lord Derby and of Bryant, and Way's spirited rendering in a
long rhymed anapæstic hexameter — a favorite with many
readers. No definitive translation of Homer is possible, for
every generation must reinterpret him in order to blend
Homeric sentiment with its own, in the measure demanded
by its taste. Of late, the majority of readers prefer the
literal prose version in slightly archaic and consciously simple
English of Lang, Leaf, and Myers. Perhaps the best course
for the student would be to use this in conjunction with Pope,
glancing now and again at Chapman for the inspiration of his
fine passages.

The study of the style and diction of Pope's *Iliad* must
start from what Matthew Arnold says of them. Pope, he
says, renders the rapidity of Homer's movement, and, to some
extent, the plainness and directness of his ideas. He is at his
best in a passage of strong emotional and oratorical movement. For, though he has not the grand style of Homer, his
literary and rhetorical manner is, in its way, well suited to
grand matters, and so he "comes off well enough so long as
he has passion, or oratory, or a great crisis to deal with."
Nevertheless, as Bentley said, it is not Homer. The rhymes

link the lines in couples, while in Homer they flow on and on. Pope indicates separation by antithesis, while Homer marks it by moving on and away. Then, though he has not Chapman's fantasticality, though he is simple in ideas like Homer, he is not like Homer simple and direct in expression. "One feels that Homer's thought has passed through a literary and rhetorical crucible, and come out highly intellectualized." He fails especially, therefore, in level passages of narration and description. In descriptions of nature, the failure is disastrous; for whereas Homer, in Wordsworth's phrase, "composes with his eye on the object," Pope writes with his eye on his style, and his endeavor is to dress up nature to advantage in an eighteenth-century costume. Starting from this general characterization, the student may observe more specifically the following traits : —

(1) Pope does not really know Greek or Homer or the primitive mind. His own early studies were all in the comparatively artificial poetry of Rome, or in those French and English writers whose inspiration is mainly Latin. So, when a passage of the *Iliad* reminds him of anything in Virgil, Dryden, or Milton, he gives to thought, imagery, or expression a Latin turn quite alien to the spirit of Homer. He employs the Latin names for the Greek gods. Hades is "Pluto's gloomy reign" (*regna*); a god is a "power" (*numen*); the Achæans are "Greece" (Grecia); Achilles "breathes the vital air" in Virgilian phrase; barley grains are the salted cake. (*salsa mola*); the ambrosial locks of Zeus are "the sacred *honors*" of his head; the "gods feast" is "the powers indulge the genial rite"; the "desire of food was spent," becomes, in Virgilian phrase "the rage of hunger was repressed," etc. Further illustrations may be grouped under the following heads : —

(*a*) Latinisms, or the use of words derived from the Latin with more or less feeling for their original force: e.g. *explore*, "look for"; *con-*

fessed, "revealed," "acknowledged"; *horrid,* "bristling"; *secure,* "without care or fear"; *expiate,* "purify"; *act,* "perform"; *decent,* "seemly," "becoming"; *desist to,* "cease from"; *selected,* "set apart"; *aspire,* "shoot up"; *impotent,* "not master of," "uncontrolled"; *merit well,* "deserve well"; *orient,* "rising"; *expire,* "emit"; *vulgar,* "common"; *contain,* "check," "hold in"; *exert,* "put forth"; *obtests,* "appeals to"; *expects,* "awaits"; *prevents,* "anticipates"; *neglect,* "not heed"; *relics,* "remains"; *produce,* "bring forth"; *certain,* "unerring"; *nerves,* "sinews"; *meditated,* "practised," "intended"; *innocent,* "harmless"; *false terrors,* "unreal," "imagined"; *resulting,* "bounding back"; *patient of,* "tolerant of"; *repugnant to,* "struggling against"; *sincere,* "unalloyed"; *office,* "service"; *strict,* "close"; *devoted,* "fated," "consecrated"; *tempt,* "make trial of"; *pest,* "bane," "ruin"; *commit,* "engage," "join in battle"; *conduct,* "guidance." To these may be added the wearisome iteration of *indulge, scene, conscious, invade, prospect, honors, monument, pledge, genial, refulgent,* etc.

(*b*) Among the explicit Virgilian reminiscences are: "breathes the vital air" (*Æn.* I. 387); "what rage can move celestial minds?" (*Æn.* I. 11); "the soul indignant seeks the realms of night," cf. 6. 679, "and Greece indignant through her seas returns" (*Æn.* 12. 952); "and trembling man sees all his labors vain" (*Æn.* 2. 305–7, cf. *Ov. Met.* I. 273); "Hector he sought, in search of Hector turn'd His eyes around, for Hector only burn'd" (*Æn.* 9. 438); "while Jove descends in sluicy sheets of rain" (*Eclogue* 7. 60); "enough is given to fame" (*Æn.* 2. 291, *sat patriæ Priamoque datum*); "around his head an iron tempest rained" (*Æn.* 12. 284); "release your smoking coursers from the car" (*Georgics,* 2. 542); "woes of which so large a part was thine," 6. 581 (*Æn.* 2. 6); "garments stiff with gold" (*Æn.* 11. 72). Cf. further notes on: I. 9–10, I. 265, I. 354, I. 614, 22. 346, 22. 417, 22. 469, 6. 114.

(*c*) Miltonic reminiscences are: "Prince thou art met"; "or bids the brazen throat of war to roar"; "beneath the whelming tide"; "native realm"; "massey"; "close consult"; "bare his red arm"; "ran purple to the main"; "curb the fiery steed"; "gloomy as night"; "fiery deluge"; "fit mast for some great admiral"; "thronged in bright arms"; "a shout that tore heaven's concave"; "native seats"; "auxiliar forces"; "his huge tempestuous sway"; "grave Nestor then in graceful act arose"; "and sacred night her awful shade extend." Cf. also I. 204 n., I. 300 n., I. 354, I. 643, I. 690, I. 711, I. 86, 6. 170.

(*d*) The reminiscences of Dryden defy enumeration. The diction of Pope's *Iliad* is essentially that of Dryden's *Virgil,* and the conception of the art of translation is the same, though Pope has realized it more brilliantly. Among the practically identical phrases common to both are: "Spires salute the sky"; "invade the sky"; "groves of lances"; "my (soul's far) better part"; "totters to her fall"; "thunderbolt of war" (Lucretius's "*belli fulmen*"); "laboring oars"; "strict embrace"; "sounding shore"; "precipitates his flight"; "female train"; "Trojan train"; "pious train"; "menial train," etc.; "blooming beauties"; "goddess of the various bow" = Iris; "power ignipotent," "forging power" = Vulcan; "blue-eyed maid" = Athena; "liquid sky"; "bird of Jove"; "queen of love"; "thundering through the field"; "watery reign"; "a sylvan scene"; "sorrow" = tears; "portents and prodigies"; "prodigal" of life, blood, or breath; "vital air"; "bare his red arm" (from Milton); "hard condition" (Shakspere); "senate" of the skies (cf. Virg. *Æn.* 10. 1, 3, 5, 97). Cf. 1. 679 n., 1. 461 n., 1. 614 n., 6. 624 n.

A few phrases also are borrowed from Dryden's version of the first book and of the Parting of Hector and Andromache. Cf. 1. 35, 1. 55, 1. 74, 1. 112, 1. 144, 1. 187, 1. 294, 1. 341, 1. 685, 6. 480, 6. 503, 6. 546–547, 6. 580, 6. 584, 6. 599.

(2) Another group of characteristics may be referred to Pope's conception of the literary dignity of the epic. To preserve this dignity he

(*a*) Softens or omits naïve, crude, or cruel touches that would offend the ears polite of eighteenth-century wits. In the comparison of Ajax to an ass, for example, the word "ass" is evaded by the paraphrase "the slow beast with heavy strength endued." The cruder details of old Phœnix's nursing of Achilles are omitted (Book IX). Other instances are: the hurling of Vulcan from heaven, 1. 760; Agamemnon's imprecations on Troy, 6. 74; the motive assigned for Glaucus's generosity, 6. 290; Helen's self-reproach, 6. 432; Achilles's rebuke of Apollo, 22. 29–30; Priam's foreboding of his fate, 22. 95–100; Hector's flight, 22. 179; Priam's ecstasy of grief, 22. 528, 24. 201, 295; his anger at his sons, 24. 332; Hecuba's wish to eat the liver of Achilles, 24. 262; Achilles's impatient warning to Priam, 24. 717. Cf. also 6. 147.

(*b*) He suggests allegorical interpretations of the gods of the mythology, and especially he strives to speak of Zeus in a manner worthy of the Supreme Being of eighteenth-century Deism. Cf. on 1. 276, 1. 556, 1. 705, 1. 760 *sqq.*, 1. 521.

(*c*). He "improves" Homer's architecture by the introduction of spires, vaulted domes, and other dignified accessories. Cf. 1. 576, 6. 304–310, 6. 371, 6. 393, 6. 490, 22. 519, 24. 204.

(*d*) He affects an un-Homeric stateliness and pseudo-dignity of expression in describing the movements and gestures of his personages, as if they were moving in a court minuet or standing for a tableau : e.g. "uprising slow," 1. 95; "slow from his seat," 1. 330; "all viewed with awe," 1. 337; "the chiefs in sullen majesty retired," 1. 401; "and oft look'd back, slow-moving o'er the strand," 1. 453; "Jove on his couch reclined his *awful* head," 1. 780; "through streets of palaces and walks of state," 6. 490; "high o'er the slain," etc., 22. 471; "slow-moving toward the shore," 22. 493; "and forth she paced majestically sad," 24. 124; "with solemn pace through various rooms he went," 24. 578; "a solemn scene," 24. 803; "majestically slow," 24. 869; "in solemn sadness and majestic grief," 9. 16, etc., etc. In this respect the racy vigor of Dryden's version of the first book is an amusing contrast to Pope. Cf. 1. 705–711 n., 1. 328 n., 1. 417 n., 1. 760 n., 1. 770 n.

(3) Whenever it seems to Pope that the literary simplicity of Homer has missed an opportunity, he adds (*a*) an ingenious conceit, (*b*) a bit of moralizing, or (*c*) a sententious maxim.

(*a*) Cf. 1. 156, 1. 215–216 n.; "as I from thee," 1. 311; 1. 394 n. 1. 457 n., 1. 509; "be still yourselves and Hector asks no more," 6. 138; "till heaps of dead alone defend her wall," 6. 411; "woes of which so large a part was thine," 6. 581; "and rise the Hector of the future age," 6. 609; "and with them turns the raised spectator's soul," 22. 216; "Achilles absent was Achilles still," 22. 418; "no — to the dogs that carcass I resign," 22. 438; "and teach him mercy when a father prays," 24. 380; "in all my equal but in misery," 24. 603. Cf. also 24. 617, 24. 778, 24. 839, 22. 87, 22. 149.

(*b*) "Rule thou thyself," 1. 373; "a dreadful lesson of exampled fate," 6. 75, 6. 329–33, 6. 290; "boasting is but an art our fears to blind," 22. 361; "while some ignobler," 22. 467; "unworthy of himself and of the dead," 22. 496; "and to his conquest add this glory more," 24. 146; 24. 193–194, 24. 530–536.

(*c*) 1. 250, "That kings are subject to the gods alone," 1. 371, 1. 383, 1. 731, 6. 427, 22. 100.

(4) The rhetorical elaboration and intellectualization of Homer's style by Pope shows itself in : —

(*a*) Ornamental periphrasis: "favoring power" = Apollo; "captive fair"; "fairest of her sex"; "bright partner of his awful reign" = Hera; "blooming beauties blessed my arms"; "the younger brothers of the pole" = the lesser gods; "the sea-green sisters" = the Nereids; "blue-eyed maid" = Athena; "sacred senate of the skies"; "indulge the genial rite" = feast; "the enamored Phrygian boy" = Paris; "sacred honors of our head" = hair; "brow's large honors" = horns; "those graceful honors" = mane; "silver-footed dame" = Thetis; "the many-colored maid" = Iris; "Jove's imperial queen" = Hera; "queen of love" = Aphrodite; "nymphs of Troy's illustrious race" = daughters of Priam; "blustering bretheren of the sky" = winds; "the purple product of the autumnal year" = grapes; "sprightly juice" = wine; "Pylian sage" or "sage protector of the Greeks" = Nestor; "the brightest of the female kind" = Helen; "tyrant of the ethereal reign" = Zeus; "fleecy care" = sheep; "fleecy winter" = snow; "the laughter-loving dame" = Aphrodite; "the strong sovereign of the plumy race" = the eagle; "patron of the bow" = Apollo; "power ignipotent" = Vulcan; "the sylvan war" = hunting, or cutting wood; "such objects as distract the fair" = corpses; "life's purple tide" = blood; "refulgent lamp of night" = the moon; "briny torrent," "infectious sorrows," "soft sorrows" = tears; "Ceres' sacred floor" = threshing-floor; "mixed the tender shower" = wept; "briny drops" = sweat; "missive wood" or "pointed death" = spear; "paths of fame" = right; "balmy blessings of the night" = sleep; "the blue languish of soft Alia's eye" = blue-eyed Alia, and so on *ad infinitum.*

(*b*) Antithesis, under which head we may include both real antithesis of thought and the favorite balanced structure of two nouns and two verbs nicely adjusted in a single line: "and for the king's offence the people died"; "the priest may pardon and the god may spare"; "we share with justice as with toil we gain"; "forced to deplore when impotent to save"; "if in my youth even these esteemed me wise; Do you, young warriors, hear my age advise"; "and pay in glory what in life you owe"; "the life which others pay, let us bestow, And give to fame what we to nature owe"; "she scorned the champion but the man she loved"; "thy love the motive and thy charms the prize"; "of lawless force shall lawless Mars complain"; "obliged the wealthy and relieved the poor"; "whose virtue charmed him as her beauty fired"; "no force could tame them, and no toil could tire." The omission of the object with the second verb is a characteristic and often a necessity of this balanced structure. Cf. Johnson's "no dangers fright him, and no labors tire." Pope's frequent use of this device gives his verse a wholly un-Homeric cast.

(*c*) The use of conventional literary metaphors now familiar to every schoolboy, but not employed by Homer: "vows be crowned"; "plough the watery plains"; "tyrant, I well deserved thy galling chain"; "tide of combat"; "where fame is reaped"; "prodigal of breath"; "my heart weeps blood"; "for he read the skies"; "the bitter dregs of fortune's cup"; "jaws of fate"; "sealed in sleep"; "dew of sleep"; "pledge" = child; "silver hairs"; "all his soul on his Patroclus fed"; "glorious face of day"; "brazen throat of war"; "a dawn of joy"; "stage of war"; "thunderbolt of war"; "iron face of war"; "thirsty sand"; "soft arms of sleep"; "discourse the medicine of the mind"; "when his earthly part shall mount in fire"; "drunk with renown"; "drown in bowls."

(*d*) The substitution of abstract for concrete forms of speech: *e.g.* "Heaven" or "the skies" for Zeus or the gods; "Greece" or "Troy" for Greeks or Trojans; "copious death" = numerous dead, 1. 534; "feathered fates," "pointed death," "feathered vengeance," "flying death" = arrows or spears; "thus spoke the prudence and the fears of age," 1. 96; "service, faith, and justice plead in vain," 1. 509; "glittering terrors" = helmet, 6. 600; "fate and fierce Achilles close behind," 22. 228; "conquest blazes," 22. 280.

(5) Other minor non-Homeric traits, as: —

(*a*) Rhetorical use of pathetic repetition: 6. 458–460, "this day — this day"; 22. 51, "stay not, stay not"; 22. 106, "this — this"; 22. 530, "O let me, let me"; 22. 507, "I fear, I fear"; 24. 105–106, "plunged — plunged"; 24. 497, "where, oh, where"; 24. 598–599, "ah think — think"; 24. 622–623, "for him — for him"; 24. 938, "which never, never"; 1. 135–137 "for this — for this"; 6. 68, "shall these, shall these"; 6. 365, "the various textures and the various dies"; 1. 544–545.

(*b*) The historical present: 1. 17, "the venerable father stands"; cf. 1. 410–415, 1. 490, 1. 622, 6. 21, 22. 207, 24. 395–396, etc.

(*c*) Use of third person for second or first: 1. 269, "descends Minerva"; 1. 444, "unmov'd as death Achilles shall remain"; 1. 394, 1. 474, "why grieves my son?" 1. 318, 6. 180, 6. 319, 6. 422, 6. 671, 6. 559, 22. 15, etc.

(*d*) Use of a resumptive phrase in loose apposition with a preceding sentence or description: 1. 432, " decent confusion "; 22. 41, " terrific glory "; 22. 638, " frugal compassion "; 24. 138, " maternal sorrows," etc. This usage is not altogether unknown to Homer.

(*e*) Omission of verb of saying before a speech: 1. 107, " to whom Peleides "; 1. 167, " then thus the king "; 22. 233, " then Pallas thus "; 22. 299, 24. 115, 24. 241, 24. 411, etc.

(*f*) Apostrophe: 22. 55, " implacable Achilles ! mightst thou be "; 24. 275, " I go, ye gods ! " 24. 307, 6. 518.

(6) The metre is the prevailing verse form of the time, the rhymed heroic couplet of five iambic feet to a verse. Pope's lines are usually quite smooth and " regular," though he admits in moderation the substitutions found in all iambic verse, rhymed or unrhymed from Shakspere and Milton down. The only points requiring notice here are : —

(*a*) The rhymes. Pope was a careless rhymer, but the pronunciation of his day differed from our own in some respects, and in some respects was unsettled. He rhymes : join with line, combine, incline, etc.; war with care, fare, and dare, etc.; revere with prayer; surveys with seas and way with sea; threat with fleet; detained with land; priest with pest; come with doom; repressed with feast; beheld with field; lost with host; deep with ship; held with shield; frown with throne; name with stream; desert with heart; decreed with dead, etc.

(*b*) In place of the couplet the triplet of three rhymes is sometimes used, 6. 322–324; 1. 355; 22. 63, 164; 24. 27, 84, 567, 685, 777, 972.

(*c*) The so-called Alexandrine line of six iambic feet is occasionally admitted, especially to wind up impressively a poetical paragraph. The name is seemingly derived from its use in old French epics on Alexander. Pope ridicules and exemplifies it thus in the *Essay on Criticism* : —

> " A needless Alexandrine ends the song
> That, like a wounded snake, drags its slow length along."

The Alexandrine of modern French poetry, though it retains the name, is really anapæstic in movement and wholly unlike Pope's line. Cf. 1. 8, " Such was the sovereign doom, and such the will of Jove "; 22. 276, " Heavy with death it sinks, and hell receives the weight "; 22. 368 ; 22. 166; 24. 779, " The rock forever lasts, the tears forever flow " — where the rhetorical intention is obvious.

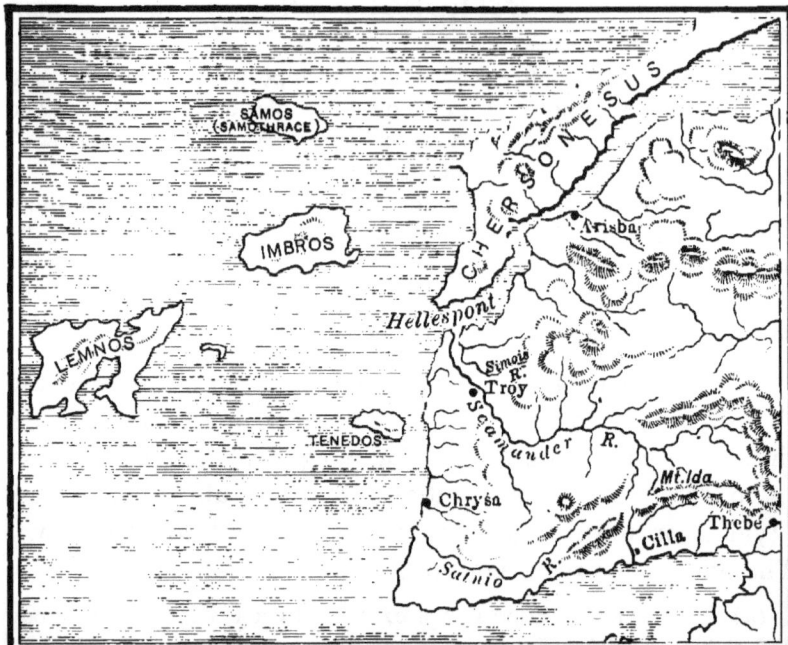

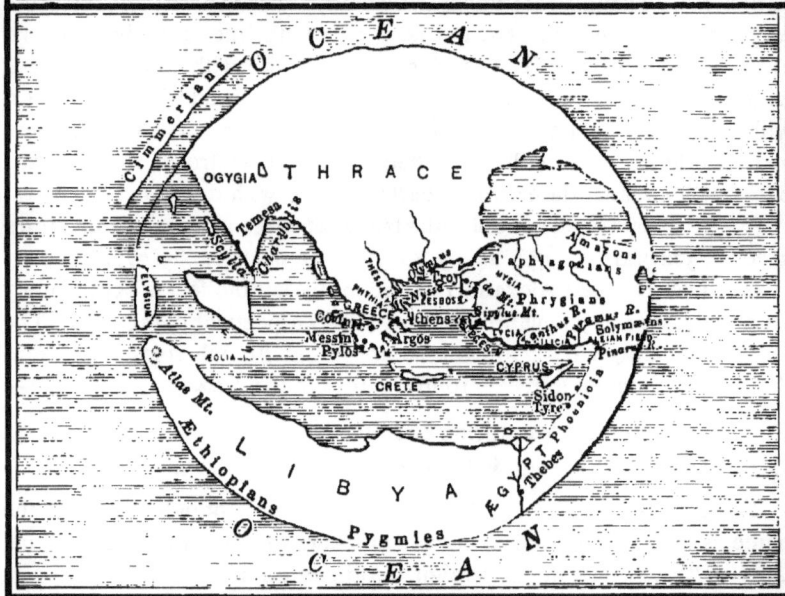

J. Flaxman and A. Schill.

THE ILIAD.

BOOK I.

THE CONTENTION OF ACHILLES AND AGAMEMNON.

ACHILLES' wrath, to Greece the direful spring
Of woes unnumber'd, heav'nly Goddess, sing !
That wrath which hurl'd to Pluto's gloomy reign
The souls of mighty chiefs untimely slain :
Whose limbs, unburied on the naked shore,   5
Devouring dogs and hungry vultures tore :
Since great Achilles and Atrides strove,
Such was the sovereign doom, and such the will of Jove !
    Declare, O Muse ! in what ill-fated hour
Sprung the fierce strife, from what offended power?   10
Latona's son a dire contagion spread,
And heap'd the camp with mountains of the dead ;

B   I

The king of men his reverend priest defied,
And, for the king's offence, the people died.

    For Chryses sought with costly gifts to gain   15
His captive daughter from the victor's chain.
Suppliant the venerable father stands ;
Apollo's awful ensigns grace his hands :
By these he begs : and, lowly bending down,
Extends the sceptre and the laurel crown.   20
He sued to all, but chief implor'd for grace
The brother-kings of Atreus' royal race :

    " Ye kings and warriors ! may your vows be crown'd,
And Troy's proud walls lie level with the ground ;
May Jove restore you, when your toils are o'er,   25
Safe to the pleasures of your native shore.
But oh ! relieve a wretched parent's pain,
And give Chryseïs to these arms again ;
If mercy fail, yet let my presents move,
And dread avenging Phœbus, son of Jove."   30

    The Greeks in shouts their joint assent declare,
The priest to reverence, and release the fair.
Not so Atrides : he, with kingly pride,
Repuls'd the sacred sire, and thus replied :

    " Hence on thy life, and fly these hostile plains,   35
Nor ask, presumptuous, what the king detains :
Hence, with thy laurel crown, and golden rod,
Nor trust too far those ensigns of thy god.
Mine is thy daughter, priest, and shall remain ;
And prayers, and tears, and bribes, shall plead in vain ; 40
Till time shall rifle every youthful grace,
And age dismiss her from my cold embrace,
In daily labours of the loom employ'd,

Or doom'd to deck the bed she once enjoy'd.
Hence then ! to Argos shall the maid retire,   45
Far from her native soil, and weeping sire."
    The trembling priest along the shore return'd,
And in the anguish of a father mourn'd.
Disconsolate, not daring to complain,
Silent he wander'd by the sounding main :   50
Till, safe at distance, to his god he prays,
The god who darts around the world his rays.
    " O Smintheus ! sprung from fair Latona's line,
Thou guardian power of Cilla the divine,
Thou source of light ! whom Tenedos adores,   55
And whose bright presence gilds thy Chrysa's shores ;
If e'er with wreaths I hung thy sacred fane,
Or fed the flames with fat of oxen slain ;
God of the silver bow ! thy shafts employ,
Avenge thy servant, and the Greeks destroy."   60
    Thus Chryses pray'd : the fav'ring power attends,
And from Olympus' lofty tops descends.
Bent was his bow, the Grecian hearts to wound ;
Fierce as he mov'd, his silver shafts resound.
Breathing revenge, a sudden night he spread,   65
And gloomy darkness roll'd around his head.
The fleet in view, he twang'd his deadly bow,
And hissing fly the feather'd fates below.
On mules and dogs th' infection first began ;
And last, the vengeful arrows fix'd in man.   70
For nine long nights, through all the dusky air
The pyres thick-flaming shot a dismal glare.
But ere the tenth revolving day was run,'
Inspir'd by Juno, Thetis' god-like son

Conven'd to council all the Grecian train;   75
For much the goddess mourn'd her heroes slain.
   Th' assembly seated, rising o'er the rest,
Achilles thus the king of men address'd :
"Why leave we not the fatal Trojan shore,
And measure back the seas we cross'd before?   80
The plague destroying whom the sword would spare,
'Tis time to save the few remains of war.
But let some prophet or some sacred sage,
Explore the cause of great Apollo's rage ;
Or learn the wasteful vengeance to remove   85
By mystic dreams, for dreams descend from Jove.
If broken vows this heavy curse have laid,
Let altars smoke, and hecatombs be paid.
So heaven aton'd shall dying Greece restore,
And Phœbus dart his burning shafts no more."   90
   He said, and sat : when Chalcas thus replied,
Chalcas the wise, the Grecian priest and guide,
That sacred seer, whose comprehensive view
The past, the present, and the future knew :
Uprising slow the venerable sage   95
Thus spoke the prudence and the fears of age :
   " Belov'd of Jove, Achilles ! would'st thou know
Why angry Phœbus bends his fatal bow?
First give thy faith, and plight a prince's word
Of sure protection, by thy pow'r and sword,   100
For I must speak what wisdom would conceal,
And truths, invidious to the great, reveal.
Bold is the task, when subjects, grown too wise,
Instruct a monarch where his error lies ;
For though we deem the short-liv'd fury past,   105

·CHRYSES· AM· MEERESSTRAND·

Friedrich Preller.

ILIAD — BOOK I., 50–68.

'Tis sure, the mighty will revenge at last."
To whom Pelides. " From thy inmost soul
Speak what thou know'st, and speak without control.
Ev'n by that god I swear, who rules the day,
To whom thy hands the vows of Greece convey,   110
And whose blest oracles thy lips declare ;
Long as Achilles breathes this vital air,
No daring Greek, of all the numerous band,
Against his priest shall lift an impious hand :
Not ev'n the chief by whom our hosts are led,   115
The king of kings, shall touch that sacred head."
Encourag'd thus, the blameless man replies :
" Nor vows unpaid, nor slighted sacrifice,
But he, our chief, provok'd the raging pest,
Apollo's vengeance for his injur'd priest.   120
Nor will the god's awaken'd fury cease,
But plagues shall spread, and funeral fires increase,
Till the great king, without a ransom paid,
To her own Chrysa send the black-ey'd maid.
Perhaps, with added sacrifice and prayer,   125
The priest may pardon, and the god may spare."
The prophet spoke ; when, with a gloomy frown,
The monarch started from his shining throne ;
Black choler fill'd his breast that boil'd with ire,
And from his eyeballs flash'd the living fire.   130
" Augur accurs'd ! denouncing mischief still,
Prophet of plagues, for ever boding ill !
Still must that tongue some wounding message bring,
And still thy priestly pride provoke thy king?
For this are Phœbus' oracles explor'd,   135
To teach the Greeks to murmur at their lord?

For this with falsehoods is my honour stain'd ;
Is heaven offended, and a priest profaned,
Because my prize, my beauteous maid, I hold,
And heav'nly charms prefer to proffer'd gold?   140
A maid, unmatch'd in manners as in face,
Skill'd in each art, and crown'd with every grace ;
Not half so dear were Clytæmnestra's charms,
When first her blooming beauties bless'd my arms.
Yet, if the gods demand her, let her sail ;   145
Our cares are only for the public weal :
Let me be deem'd the hateful cause of all,
And suffer, rather than my people fall.
The prize, the beauteous prize, I will resign,
So dearly valued, and so justly mine.   150
But since for common good I yield the fair,
My private loss let grateful Greece repair ;
Nor unrewarded let your prince complain,
That he alone has fought and bled in vain."
    " Insatiate king ! " (Achilles thus replies)   155
" Fond of the pow'r, but fonder of the prize !
Wouldst thou the Greeks their lawful prey should yield,
The due reward of many a well-fought field?
The spoils of cities razed, and warriors slain,
We share with justice, as with toil we gain : ·   160
But to resume whate'er thy avarice craves,
(That trick of tyrants) may be borne by slaves.
Yet if our chief for plunder only fight,
The spoils of Ilion shall thy loss requite,
Whene'er, by Jove's decree, our conqu'ring pow'rs   165
Shall humble to the dust her lofty tow'rs."
    Then thus the king.   " Shall I my prize resign

With tame content, and thou possess'd of thine?
Great as thou art, and like a god in fight,
Think not to rob me of a soldier's right.   170
At thy demand shall I restore the maid?
First let the just equivalent be paid;
Such as a king might ask; and let it be
A treasure worthy her, and worthy me.
Or grant me this, or with a monarch's claim   175
This hand shall seize some other captive dame.
The mighty Ajax shall his prize resign,
Ulysses' spoils, or e'en thy own be mine.
The man who suffers, loudly may complain;
And rage he may, but he shall rage in vain.   180
But this when time requires.   It now remains
We launch a bark to plough the watery plains,
And waft the sacrifice to Chrysa's shores,
With chosen pilots, and with lab'ring oars.
Soon shall the fair the sable ship ascend,   185
And some deputed prince the charge attend.
This Creta's king, or Ajax shall fulfil,
Or wise Ulysses see perform'd our will;
Or, if our royal pleasure shall ordain,
Achilles' self conduct her o'er the main;   190
Let fierce Achilles, dreadful in his rage,
The god propitiate, and the pest assuage."
    At this, Pelides, frowning stern, replied:
"O tyrant, arm'd with insolence and pride!
Inglorious slave to interest, ever join'd   195
With fraud, unworthy of a royal mind!
What gen'rous Greek, obedient to thy word,
Shall form an ambush, or shall lift the sword?

What cause have I to war at thy decree?
The distant Trojans never injured me :   200
To Phthia's realms no hostile troops they led ;
Safe in her vales my warlike coursers fed ;
Far hence remov'd, the hoarse-resounding main,
And walls of rocks, secure my native reign,
Whose fruitful soil luxuriant harvests grace,   205
Rich in her fruits, and in her martial race.
Hither we sail'd, a voluntary throng,
T' avenge a private not a public wrong :
What else to Troy th' assembled nations draws,
But thine, ungrateful, and thy brother's cause?   210
Is this the pay our blood and toils deserve,
Disgraced and injur'd by the man we serve?
And dar'st thou threat to snatch my prize away,
Due to the deeds of many a dreadful day?
A prize as small, O tyrant ! match'd with thine,   215
As thy own actions if compar'd to mine.
Thine in each conquest is the wealthy prey,
Though mine the sweat and danger of the day.
Some trivial present to my ships I bear,
Or barren praises pay the wounds of war.   220
But know, proud monarch, I'm thy slave no more :
My fleet shall waft me to Thessalia's shore.
Left by Achilles on the Trojan plain,
What spoils, what conquests, shall Atrides gain?"
    To this the king: " Fly, mighty warrior ! fly, 225
Thy aid we need not, and thy threats defy :
There want not chiefs in such a cause to fight,
And Jove himself shall guard a monarch's right.
Of all the kings (the gods' distinguish'd care)

To pow'r superior none such hatred bear ;   230
Strife and debate thy restless soul employ,
And wars and horrors are thy savage joy.
If thou hast strength, 'twas Heav'n that strength bestow'd,
For know, vain man ! thy valour is from God.
Haste, launch thy vessels, fly with speed away,   235
Rule thy own realms with arbitrary sway :
I heed thee not, but prize at equal rate
Thy short-liv'd friendship, and thy groundless hate.
Go, threat thy earth-born Myrmidons ; but here
'Tis mine to threaten, prince, and thine to fear.   240
Know, if the god the beauteous dame demand,
My bark shall waft her to her native land ;
But then prepare, imperious prince ! prepare,
Fierce as thou art, to yield thy captive fair :
E'en in thy tent I'll seize the blooming prize,   245
Thy lov'd Briseïs, with the radiant eyes.
Hence shalt thou prove my might, and curse the hour,
Thou stood'st a rival of imperial pow'r ;
And hence to all our host it shall be known
That kings are subject to the gods alone."   250
    Achilles heard, with grief and rage oppress'd ;
His heart swell'd high, and labour'd in his breast.
Distracting thoughts by turns his bosom rul'd,
Now fir'd by wrath, and now by reason cool'd :
That prompts his hand to draw the deadly sword,   255
Force thro' the Greeks, and pierce their haughty lord ;
This whispers soft his vengeance to control
And calm the rising tempest of his soul.
Just as in anguish of suspense he stay'd,
While half unsheath'd appear'd the glitt'ring blade,   260

Minerva swift descended from above,
Sent by the sister and the wife of Jove ;
(For both the princes claim'd her equal care ;)
Behind she stood, and by the golden hair
Achilles seiz'd ; to him alone confess'd ;   265
A sable cloud conceal'd her from the rest.
He sees, and sudden to the goddess cries,
Known by the flames that sparkle from her eyes :
  " Descends Minerva, in her guardian care,
A heav'nly witness of the wrongs I bear   270
From Atreus' son?   Then let those eyes that view
The daring crime, behold the vengeance too."
  " Forbear ! " (the progeny of Jove replies)
" To calm thy fury I forsake the skies :
Let great Achilles, to the gods resign'd,   275
To reason yield the empire o'er his mind.
By awful Juno this command is giv'n ;
The king and you are both the care of heav'n.
The force of keen reproaches let him feel,
But sheathe, obedient, thy revenging steel.   280
For I pronounce (and trust a heav'nly pow'r)
Thy injur'd honour has its fated hour,
When the proud monarch shall thy arms implore,
And bribe thy friendship with a boundless store.
Then let revenge no longer bear the sway,   285
Command thy passions, and the gods obey."
  To her Pelides : " With regardful ear,
'Tis just, O goddess ! I thy dictates hear.
Hard as it is, my vengeance I suppress :
Those who revere the gods, the gods will bless."   290
He said, observant of the blue-ey'd maid ;

Then in the sheath return'd the shining blade.
The goddess swift to high Olympus flies,
And joins the sacred senate of the skies.
    Nor yet the rage his boiling breast forsook,   295
Which thus redoubling on Atrides broke :
" O monster ! mix'd of insolence and fear,
Thou dog in forehead, but in heart a deer !
When wert thou known in ambush'd fights to dare,
Or nobly face the horrid front of war ?   300
'Tis ours, the chance of fighting fields to try,
Thine to look on, and bid the valiant die.
So much 'tis safer through the camp to go,
And rob a subject, than despoil a foe.
Scourge of thy people, violent and base !   305
Sent in Jove's anger on a slavish race,
Who, lost to sense of generous freedom past,
Are tam'd to wrongs, or this had been thy last.
Now by this sacred sceptre hear me swear,
Which never more shall leaves or blossoms bear,   310
Which, sever'd from the trunk (as I from thee)
On the bare mountains left its parent tree ;
This sceptre, form'd by temper'd steel to prove
An ensign of the delegates of Jove,
From whom the pow'r of laws and justice springs :   315
(Tremendous oath ! inviolate to kings) :
By this I swear, when bleeding Greece again
Shall call Achilles, she shall call in vain.
When, flush'd with slaughter, Hector comes to spread
The purpled shore with mountains of the dead,   320
Then shalt thou mourn th' affront thy madness gave,
Forced to deplore, when impotent to save :

Then rage in bitterness of soul, to know
'This act has made the bravest Greek thy foe."

He spoke ; and furious hurl'd against the ground   325
His sceptre starr'd with golden studs around ;
Then sternly silent sat.   With like disdain,
The raging king return'd his frowns again.

To calm their passion with the words of age,
Slow from his seat arose the Pylian sage.   330
Experienced Nestor, in persuasion skill'd ;
Words sweet as honey from his lips distill'd :
Two generations now had pass'd away,
Wise by his rules, and happy by his sway ;
Two ages o'er his native realm he reign'd,   335
And now th' example of the third remain'd.
All view'd with awe the venerable man ;
Who thus, with mild benevolence, began :

" What shame, what woe is this to Greece ! what joy
To Troy's proud monarch, and the friends of Troy !   340
That adverse gods commit to stern debate
The best, the bravest of the Grecian state.
Young as you are, this youthful heat restrain,
Nor think your Nestor's years and wisdom vain.
A godlike race of heroes once I knew,   345
Such as no more these aged eyes shall view !
Lives there a chief to match Pirithous' fame,
Dryas the bold, or Ceneus' deathless name ;
Theseus, endued with more than mortal might,
Or Polyphemus, like the gods in fight?   350
With these of old to toils of battle bred,
In early youth my hardy days I led ;
Fir'd with the thirst which virtuous envy breeds,

And smit with love of honourable deeds.
Strongest of men, they pierced the mountain boar,   355
Ranged the wild deserts red with monsters' gore,
And from their hills the shaggy Centaurs tore.
Yet these with soft persuasive arts I sway'd;
When Nestor spoke, they listen'd and obey'd.
If in my youth, e'en these esteem'd me wise,   360
Do you, young warriors, hear my age advise.
Atrides, seize not on the beauteous slave;
That prize the Greeks by common suffrage gave:
Nor thou, Achilles, treat our prince with pride;
Let kings be just, and sov'reign pow'r preside: 365
Thee, the first honours of the war adorn,
Like gods in strength, and of a goddess born;
Him, awful majesty exalts above
The pow'rs of earth, and sceptred sons of Jove.
Let both unite with well-consenting mind,   370
So shall authority with strength be join'd.
Leave me, O king! to calm Achilles' rage;
Rule thou thyself, as more advanced in age.
Forbid it, gods! Achilles should be lost,
The pride of Greece, and bulwark of our host."   375
  This said, he ceas'd: the king of men replies:
"Thy years are awful, and thy words are wise.
But that imperious, that unconquer'd soul,
No laws can limit, no respect control:
Before his pride must his superiors fall,   380
His word the law, and he the lord of all?
Him must our hosts, our chiefs, ourself obey?
What king can bear a rival in his sway?
Grant that the gods his matchless force have giv'n;

Has foul reproach a privilege from heav'n?"   385
   Here on the monarch's speech Achilles broke,
And furious, thus, and interrupting, spoke:
"Tyrant, I well deserv'd thy galling chain,
To live thy slave, and still to serve in vain,
Should I submit to each unjust decree: 390
Command thy vassals, but command not me.
Seize on Briseïs, whom the Grecians doom'd
My prize of war, yet tamely see resum'd;
And seize secure; no more Achilles draws
His conqu'ring sword in any woman's cause.   395
The gods command me to forgive the past;
But let this first invasion be the last:
For know, thy blood, when next thou dar'st invade,
Shall stream in vengeance on my reeking blade."
   At this they ceas'd; the stern debate expir'd: 400
The chiefs in sullen majesty retir'd.
   Achilles with Patroclus took his way,
Where near his tents his hollow vessels lay.
Meantime Atrides launch'd with numerous oars
A well-rigg'd ship for Chrysa's sacred shores: 405
High on the deck was fair Chryseïs placed,
And sage Ulysses with the conduct graced:
Safe in her sides the hecatomb they stow'd,
Then, swiftly sailing, cut the liquid road.
   The host to expiate next the king prepares,   410
With pure lustrations and with solemn pray'rs.
Wash'd by the briny wave, the pious train
Are cleans'd; and cast th' ablutions in the main.
Along the shore whole hecatombs were laid,
And bulls and goats to Phœbus' altars paid.   415

The sable fumes in curling spires arise,
And waft their grateful odours to the skies.
    The army thus in sacred rites engaged,
Atrides still with deep resentment raged.
To wait his will two sacred heralds stood,   420
Talthybius and Eurybates the good.
"Haste to the fierce Achilles' tent," (he cries,)
"Thence bear Briseïs as our royal prize :
Submit he must ; or, if they will not part,
Ourself in arms shall tear her from his heart."   425
    Th' unwilling heralds act their lord's commands ;
Pensive they walk along the barren sands :
Arriv'd, the hero in his tent they find,
With gloomy aspect, on his arm reclin'd.
At awful distance long they silent stand,   430
Loth to advance, or speak their hard command ;
Decent confusion !   This the godlike man
Perceiv'd, and thus with accent mild began :
    "With leave and honour enter our abodes,
Ye sacred ministers of men and gods !   435
I know your message ; by constraint you came ;
Not you, but your imperious lord, I blame.
Patroclus, haste, the fair Briseïs bring ;
Conduct my captive to the haughty king.
But witness, heralds, and proclaim my vow,   440
Witness to gods above, and men below !
But first, and loudest, to your prince declare,
That lawless tyrant whose commands you bear ;
Unmov'd as death Achilles shall remain,
Though prostrate Greece should bleed at every vein : 445
The raging chief in frantic passion lost,

Blind to himself, and useless to his host,
Unskill'd to judge the future by the past,
In blood and slaughter shall repent at last."
　　Patroclus now th' unwilling beauty brought;   450
She, in soft sorrows, and in pensive thought,
Pass'd silent, as the heralds held her hand,
And oft look'd back, slow-moving o'er the strand.
　　Not so his loss the fierce Achilles bore;
But sad retiring to the sounding shore,   455
O'er the wild margin of the deep he hung,
That kindred deep from whence his mother sprung;
There, bath'd in tears of anger and disdain,
Thus loud lamented to the stormy main:
　　"O parent goddess! since in early bloom   460
Thy son must fall, by too severe a doom;
Sure, to so short a race of glory born,
Great Jove in justice should this span adorn.
Honour and fame at least the Thunderer owed;
And ill he pays the promise of a god,   465
If yon proud monarch thus thy son defies,
Obscures my glories, and resumes my prize."
　　Far in the deep recesses of the main,
Where aged Ocean holds his watery reign,
The goddess-mother heard.   The waves divide;   470
And like a mist she rose above the tide;
Beheld him mourning on the naked shores,
And thus the sorrows of his soul explores:
" Why grieves my son? thy anguish let me share,
Reveal the cause, and trust a parent's care."   475
　　He deeply sighing said: " To tell my woe,
Is but to mention what too well you know.

From Thebè, sacred to Apollo's name,
(Eëtion's realm,) our conqu'ring army came,
With treasure loaded and triumphant spoils,   480
Whose just division crown'd the soldier's toils ;
But bright Chryseïs, heav'nly prize ! was led
By vote selected to the general's bed.
The priest of Phœbus sought by gifts to gain
His beauteous daughter from the victor's chain ;   485
The fleet he reach'd, and, lowly bending down,
Held forth the sceptre and the laurel crown,
Entreating all ; but chief implor'd for grace
The brother-kings of Atreus' royal race :
The gen'rous Greeks their joint consent declare,   490
The priest to reverence, and release the fair.
Not so Atrides : he, with wonted pride,
The sire insulted, and his gifts denied :
Th' insulted sire (his god's peculiar care)
To Phœbus pray'd, and Phœbus heard the pray'r :   495
A dreadful plague ensues ; th' avenging darts
Incessant fly, and pierce the Grecian hearts.
A prophet then, inspir'd by heaven, arose,
And points the crime, and thence derives the woes :
Myself the first th' assembled chiefs incline   500
T' avert the vengeance of the pow'r divine ;
Then, rising in his wrath, the monarch storm'd ;
Incens'd he threaten'd, and his threats perform'd :
The fair Chryseïs to her sire was sent,
With offer'd gifts to make the god relent ;   505
But now he seiz'd Briseïs' heav'nly charms,
And of my valour's prize defrauds my arms,
Defrauds the votes of all the Grecian train ;

c

And service, faith, and justice, plead in vain.
But, goddess ! thou thy suppliant son attend,   510
To high Olympus' shining court ascend,
Urge all the ties to former service ow'd,
And sue for vengeance to the thundering god.
Oft hast thou triumph'd in the glorious boast
That thou stood'st forth, of all the ethereal host,   515
When bold rebellion shook the realms above,
Th' undaunted guard of cloud-compelling Jove.
When the bright partner of his awful reign,
The warlike maid, and monarch of the main,
The traitor-gods, by mad ambition driv'n,   520
Durst threat with chains th' omnipotence of heav'n.
Then call'd by thee, the monster Titan came ;
(Whom gods Briareus, men Ægeon name ;)
Through wondering skies enormous stalk'd along ;
Not he that shakes the solid earth so strong :   525
With giant-pride at Jove's high throne he stands,
And brandish'd round him all his hundred hands.
Th' affrighted gods confess'd their awful lord,
They dropp'd the fetters, trembled and ador'd.
This, goddess, this to his rememb'rance call,   530
Embrace his knees, at his tribunal fall ;
Conjure him far to drive the Grecian train,
To hurl them headlong to their fleet and main,
To heap the shores with copious death and bring
The Greeks to know the curse of such a king :   535
Let Agamemnon lift his haughty head
O'er all his wide dominion of the dead,
And mourn in blood, that e'er he durst disgrace
The boldest warrior of the Grecian race."

" Unhappy son ! " (fair Thetis thus replies,   540
While tears celestial trickle from her eyes,)
" Why have I borne thee with a mother's throes,
To fates averse, and nurs'd for future woes?
So short a space the light of heav'n to view !
So short a space ! and fill'd with sorrow too !   545
O might a parent's careful wish prevail,
Far, far from Ilion should thy vessels sail,
And thou, from camps remote, the danger shun,
Which now, alas ! too nearly threats my son.
Yet (what I can) to move thy suit I'll go   550
To great Olympus crown'd with fleecy snow.
Meantime, secure within thy ships from far,
Behold the field, nor mingle in the war.
The sire of gods, and all th' ethereal train,
On the warm limits of the farthest main,   555
Now mix with mortals, nor disdain to grace
The feasts of Æthiopia's blameless race :
Twelve days the powers indulge the genial rite,
Returning with the twelfth revolving light.
Then will I mount the brazen dome, and move   560
The high tribunal of immortal Jove."
    The goddess spoke : the rolling waves unclose ;
Then down the deep she plunged, from whence she rose,
And left him sorrowing on the lonely coast
In wild resentment for the fair he lost.   565
    In Chrysa's port now sage Ulysses rode ;
Beneath the deck the destin'd victims stow'd :
The sails they furl'd, they lash'd the mast aside,
And dropp'd their anchors, and the pinnace tied.
Next on the shore their hecatomb they land,   570

Chryseïs last descending on the strand.
Her, thus returning from the furrow'd main,
Ulysses led to Phœbus' sacred fane ;
Where at his solemn altar, as the maid
He gave to Chryses, thus the hero said :   575
  " Hail, reverend priest ! to Phœbus' awful dome
A suppliant I from great Atrides come :
Unransom'd here receive the spotless fair ;
Accept the hecatomb the Greeks prepare ;
And may thy god, who scatters darts around,   580
Aton'd by sacrifice, desist to wound."
  At this the sire embraced the maid again,
So sadly lost, so lately sought in vain.
Then near the altar of the darting king,
Dispos'd in rank their hecatomb they bring :   585
With water purify their hands, and take
The sacred offering of the salted cake ;
While thus with arms devoutly rais'd in air,
And solemn voice, the priest directs his prayer :
  " God of the silver bow, thy ear incline,   590
Whose power encircles Cilla the divine ;
Whose sacred eye thy Tenedos surveys,
And gilds fair Chrysa with distinguish'd rays !
If, fir'd to vengeance at thy priest's request,
Thy direful darts inflict the raging pest ;   595
Once more attend ! avert the wasteful woe,
And smile propitious, and unbend thy bow."
  So Chryses pray'd.   Apollo heard his prayer :
And now the Greeks their hecatomb prepare ;
Between their horns the salted barley threw,   600
And with their heads to heaven the victims slew :

The limbs they sever from th' inclosing hide ;
The thighs, selected to the gods, divide :
On these, in double cauls involv'd with art,
The choicest morsels lay from every part.   605
The priest himself before his altar stands,
And burns the offering with his holy hands,
Pours the black wine, and sees the flames aspire ;
The youths with instruments surround the fire :
The thighs thus sacrificed, and entrails drest,   610
Th' assistants part, transfix, and roast the rest :
Then spread the tables, the repast prepare,
Each takes his seat, and each receives his share.
When now the rage of hunger was repress'd,
With pure libations they conclude the feast ;   615
The youths with wine the copious goblets crown'd,
And, pleas'd, dispense the flowing bowls around.
With hymns divine the joyous banquet ends,
The Pæans lengthen'd till the sun descends :
The Greeks, restor'd, the grateful notes prolong :   620
Apollo listens, and approves the song.
    'Twas night ; the chiefs beside their vessel lie,
Till rosy morn had purpled o'er the sky :
Then launch, and hoist the mast ; indulgent gales,
Supplied by Phœbus, fill the swelling sails ;   625
The milk-white canvas bellying as they blow,
The parted ocean foams and roars below :
Above the bounding billows swift they flew,
Till now the Grecian camp appear'd in view.
Far on the beach they haul their barks to land,   630
(The crooked keel divides the yellow sand,)
Then part, where stretch'd along the winding bay

The ships and tents in mingled prospect lay.
  But, raging still, amidst his navy sat
The stern Achilles, steadfast in his hate ;   635
Nor mix'd in combat, nor in council join'd ;
But wasting cares lay heavy on his mind :
In his black thoughts revenge and slaughter roll,
And scenes of blood rise dreadful in his soul.
  Twelve days were past, and now the dawning light 640
The gods had summon'd to th' Olympian height :
Jove, first ascending from the watery bowers,
Leads the long order of ethereal powers.
When like the morning mist, in early day,
Rose from the flood the daughter of the sea ;   645
And to the seats divine her flight address'd.
There, far apart, and high above the rest,
The Thunderer sat ; where old Olympus shrouds
His hundred heads in heaven, and props the clouds.
Suppliant the goddess stood : one hand she placed   650
Beneath his beard, and one his knees embraced.
"If e'er, O father of the gods !" she said,
" My words could please thee, or my actions aid ;
Some marks of honour on thy son bestow,
And pay in glory what in life you owe.   655
Fame is at least by heavenly promise due
To life so short and now dishonour'd too.
Avenge this wrong, oh ever just and wise !
Let Greece be humbled, and the Trojans rise ;
Till the proud king, and all th' Achaian race   660
Shall heap with honours him they now disgrace."
  Thus Thetis spoke, but Jove in silence held
The sacred counsels of his breast conceal'd.

Not so repuls'd, the goddess closer press'd,
Still grasp'd his knees, and urged the dear request.　665
" O sire of gods and men ! thy suppliant hear,
Refuse, or grant ; for what has Jove to fear ?
Or, oh ! declare, of all the powers above,
Is wretched Thetis least the care of Jove ? "
　She said, and sighing thus the god replies,　670
Who rolls the thunder o'er the vaulted skies :
　" What hast thou ask'd ?　Ah why should Jove engage
In foreign contests, and domestic rage,
The gods' complaints, and Juno's fierce alarms,
While I, too partial, aid the Trojan arms ?　675
Go, lest the haughty partner of my sway
With jealous eyes thy close access survey ;
But part in peace, secure thy prayer is sped :
Witness the sacred honours of our head,
The nod that ratifies the will divine,　680
The faithful, fix'd, irrevocable sign ;
This seals thy suit, and this fulfils thy vows — "
He spoke, and awful bends his sable brows ;
Shakes his ambrosial curls, and gives the nod ;
The stamp of fate, and sanction of the god :　685
High heaven with trembling the dread signal took,
And all Olympus to the centre shook.
　Swift to the seas profound the goddess flies,
Jove to his starry mansion in the skies.
The shining synod of th' immortals wait　690
The coming god, and from their thrones of state
Arising silent, rapt in holy fear,
Before the majesty of heaven appear.
Trembling they stand, while Jove assumes the throne,

All, but the god's imperious queen alone :   695
Late had she view'd the silver-footed dame,
And all her passions kindled into flame.
" Say, artful manager of heaven," (she cries,)
Who now partakes the secrets of the skies?
Thy Juno knows not the decrees of fate,   700
In vain the partner of imperial state.
What fav'rite goddess then those cares divides,
Which Jove in prudence from his consort hides?"
    To this the Thunderer : " Seek not thou to find
The sacred counsels of almighty mind :   705
Involv'd in darkness lies the great decree,
Nor can the depths of fate be pierced by thee.
What fits thy knowledge, thou the first shalt know :
The first of gods above and men below :
But thou, nor they, shall search the thoughts that roll 710
Deep in the close recesses of my soul."
    Full on the sire, the goddess of the skies
Roll'd the large orbs of her majestic eyes,
And thus return'd : " Austere Saturnius, say,
From whence this wrath, or who controls thy sway?   715
Thy boundless will, for me, remains in force,
And all thy counsels take the destin'd course.
But 'tis for Greece I fear : for late was seen
In close consult the silver-footed queen.
Jove to his Thetis nothing could deny,   720
Nor was the signal vain that shook the sky.
What fatal favour has the goddess won,
To grace her fierce inexorable son?
Perhaps in Grecian blood to drench the plain,
And glut his vengeance with my people slain."   725

Then thus the god : " Oh restless fate of pride,
That strives to learn what heaven resolves to hide ;
Vain is the search, presumptuous and abhorr'd,
Anxious to thee, and odious to thy lord.
Let this suffice : th' immutable decree 730
No force can shake : what *is*, that *ought* to be.
Goddess submit, nor dare our will withstand,
But dread the power of this avenging hand ;
Th' united strength of all the gods above
In vain resists th' omnipotence of Jove." 735
    The Thunderer spoke, nor durst the queen reply ;
A reverend horror silenced all the sky.
The feast disturb'd, with sorrow Vulcan saw
His mother menaced, and the gods in awe ;
Peace at his heart, and pleasure his design, 740
Thus interpos'd the architect divine :
" The wretched quarrels of the mortal state
Are far unworthy, gods ! of your debate :
Let men their days in senseless strife employ,
We, in eternal peace, and constant joy. 745
Thou, goddess-mother, with our sire comply,
Nor break the sacred union of the sky :
Lest, rous'd to rage, he shake the blest abodes,
Launch the red lightning, and dethrone the gods.
If you submit, the Thunderer stands appeas'd ; 750
The gracious power is willing to be pleas'd."
    Thus Vulcan spoke ; and, rising with a bound,
The double bowl with sparkling nectar crown'd,
Which held to Juno in a cheerful way,
" Goddess," (he cried,) " be patient and obey. 755
Dear as you are, if Jove his arm extend,

I can but grieve, unable to defend.
What god so daring in your aid to move,
Or lift his hand against the force of Jove?
Once in your cause I felt his matchless might,   760
Hurl'd headlong downward from th' ethereal height;
Toss'd all the day in rapid circles round;
Nor, till the sun descended, touch'd the ground:
Breathless I fell, in giddy motion lost;
The Sinthians rais'd me on the Lemnian coast."   765

    He said, and to her hands the goblet heav'd,
Which, with a smile, the white-arm'd queen receiv'd.
Then to the rest he fill'd; and, in his turn,
Each to his lips applied the nectar'd urn.
Vulcan with awkward grace his office plies,   770
And unextinguish'd laughter shakes the skies.

    Thus the blest gods the genial day prolong,
In feasts ambrosial, and celestial song.
Apollo tun'd the lyre; the muses round
With voice alternate aid the silver sound.   775
Meantime the radiant sun, to mortal sight
Descending swift, roll'd down the rapid light.
Then to their starry domes the gods depart,
The shining monuments of Vulcan's art:
Jove on his couch reclin'd his awful head,   780
And Juno slumber'd on the golden bed.

J. Flaxman and A. Schill.

BOOK VI.

THE EPISODES OF GLAUCUS AND DIOMED, AND OF HECTOR AND ANDROMACHE.

Now heaven forsakes the fight; th' immortals yield
To human force and human skill the field :
Dark showers of javelins fly from foes to foes ;
Now here, now there, the tide of combat flows ;
While Troy's fam'd streams, that bound the deathful
    plain   5
On either side, run purple to the main.
    Great Ajax first to conquest led the way,
Broke the thick ranks, and turn'd the doubtful day.
The Thracian Acamas his falchion found,
And hew'd th' enormous giant to the ground ;   10
His thundering arm a deadly stroke impress'd
Where the black horse-hair nodded o'er his crest :

27

Fix'd in his front the brazen weapon lies,
And seals in endless shades his swimming eyes.
   Next Teuthras' son distain'd the sands with blood,   15
Axylus, hospitable, rich, and good :
In fair Arisba's walls (his native place)
He held his seat ; a friend to human race.
Fast by the road, his ever-open door
Obliged the wealthy, and reliev'd the poor.   20
To stern Tydides now he falls a prey,
No friend to guard him in the dreadful day !
Breathless the good man fell, and by his side
His faithful servant, old Calesius, died.
   By great Euryalus was Dresus slain,   25
And next he laid Opheltius on the plain.
Two twins were near, bold, beautiful, and young,
From a fair Naiad and Bucolion sprung :
(Laomedon's white flocks Bucolion fed,
That monarch's first-born by a foreign bed ;   30
In secret woods he won the Naiad's grace,
And two fair infants crown'd his strong embrace :)
Here dead they lay in all their youthful charms ;
The ruthless victor stripp'd their shining arms.
   Astyalus by Polypœtes fell ;   35
Ulysses' spear Pidytes sent to hell ;
By Teucer's shaft brave Aretaön bled,
And Nestor's son laid stern Ablerus dead ;
Great Agamemnon, leader of the brave,
The mortal wound of rich Elatus gave,   40
Who held in Pedasus his proud abode,
And till'd the banks where silver Satnio flow'd.
Melanthius by Eurypylus was slain ;

And Phylacus from Leitus flies in vain.
    Unbless'd Adrastus next at mercy lies   45
Beneath the Spartan spear, a living prize.
Scar'd with the din and tumult of the fight,
His headlong steeds, precipitate in flight,
Rush'd on a tamarisk's strong trunk, and broke
The shatter'd chariot from the crooked yoke: 50
Wide o'er the field, resistless as the wind,
For Troy they fly, and leave their lord behind.
Prone on his face he sinks beside the wheel;
Atrides o'er him shakes his vengeful steel;
The fallen chief in suppliant posture press'd   55
The victor's knees, and thus his prayer address'd:
    "Oh, spare my youth, and for the life I owe
Large gifts of price my father shall bestow:
When fame shall tell, that, not in battle slain,
Thy hollow ships his captive son detain,   60
Rich heaps of brass shall in thy tent be told,
And steel well temper'd, and persuasive gold."
    He said: compassion touch'd the hero's heart;
He stood suspended with the lifted dart:
As pity pleaded for his vanquish'd prize,   65
Stern Agamemnon swift to vengeance flies,
And furious thus: "Oh impotent of mind!
Shall these, shall these, Atrides' mercy find?
Well hast thou known proud Troy's perfidious land,
And well her natives merit at thy hand!   70
Not one of all the race, nor sex, nor age,
Shall save a Trojan from our boundless rage:
Ilion shall perish whole, and bury all;
Her babes, her infants at the breast, shall fall.

A dreadful lesson of exampled fate,   75
To warn the nations, and to curb the great.
   The monarch spoke; the words, with warmth address'd,
To rigid justice steel'd his brother's breast.
Fierce from his knees the hapless chief he thrust;
The monarch's javelin stretch'd him in the dust.   80
Then, pressing with his foot his panting heart,
Forth from the slain he tugg'd the reeking dart.
Old Nestor saw, and rous'd the warriors' rage;
"Thus, heroes! thus the vigorous combat wage!
No son of Mars descend, for servile gains,   85
To touch the booty, while a foe remains.
Behold yon glittering host, your future spoil!
First gain the conquest, then reward the toil."
   And now had Greece eternal fame acquir'd,
And frighted Troy within her walls retir'd;   90
Had not sage Helenus her state redress'd,
Taught by the gods that mov'd his sacred breast:
Where Hector stood, with great Æneas join'd,
The seer reveal'd the counsels of his mind:
   "Ye generous chiefs! on whom th' immortals lay 95
The cares and glories of this doubtful day,
On whom your aids, your country's hopes depend
Wise to consult, and active to defend!
Here, at our gates, your brave efforts unite,
Turn back the routed, and forbid the flight;   100
Ere yet their wives' soft arms the cowards gain,
The sport and insult of the hostile train.
When your commands have hearten'd every band,
Ourselves, here fixed, will make the dang'rous stand;
Press'd as we are, and sore of former fight,   105

These straits demand our last remains of might.
Meanwhile, thou, Hector, to the town retire,
And teach our mother what the gods require :
Direct the queen to lead th' assembled train
Of Troy's chief matrons to Minerva's fane ;   110
Unbar the sacred gates, and seek the power
With offer'd vows, in Ilion's topmost tower.
The largest mantle her rich wardrobes hold,
Most priz'd for art, and labour'd o'er with gold,
Before the goddess' honour'd knees be spread ;   115
And twelve young heifers to her altars led.
If so the power, aton'd by fervent prayer,
Our wives, our infants, and our city spare,
And far avert Tydides' wasteful ire,
That mows whole troops, and makes all Troy retire.   120
Not thus Achilles taught our hosts to dread,
Sprung though he was from more than mortal bed ;
Not thus resistless rul'd the stream of fight,
In rage unbounded, and unmatch'd in might."
    Hector obedient heard ; and, with a bound,   125
Leap'd from his trembling chariot to the ground ;
Through all his host, inspiring force, he flies,
And bids the thunder of the battle rise.
With rage recruited the bold Trojans glow,
And turn the tide of conflict on the foe :   130
Fierce in the front he shakes two dazzling spears ;
All Greece recedes, and midst her triumph fears :
Some god, they thought, who rul'd the fate of wars,
Shot down avenging, from the vault of stars.
    Then thus, aloud : " Ye dauntless Dardans, hear !   135
And you whom distant nations send to war ;

Be mindful of the strength your fathers bore ;
Be still yourselves, and Hector asks no more.
One hour demands me in the Trojan wall,
To bid our altars flame, and victims fall :   140
Nor shall, I trust, the matrons' holy train,
And reverend elders, seek the gods in vain."

   This said, with ample strides the hero pass'd ;
The shield's large orb behind his shoulder cast,
His neck o'ershading, to his ankle hung ;   145
And as he march'd the brazen buckler rung.

   Now paus'd the battle, (godlike Hector gone,)
When daring Glaucus and great Tydeus' son
Between both armies met ; the chiefs from far
Observ'd each other, and had mark'd for war.   150
Near as they drew, Tydides thus began :
" What art thou, boldest of the race of man ?
Our eyes, till now, that aspect ne'er beheld,
Where fame is reap'd amid th' embattled field ;
Yet far before the troops thou dar'st appear,   155
And meet a lance the fiercest heroes fear.
Unhappy they, and born of luckless sires,
Who tempt our fury when Minerva fires !
But if from heaven, celestial, thou descend,
Know, with immortals we no more contend.   160
Not long Lycurgus view'd the golden light,
That daring man who mix'd with gods in fight ;
Bacchus, and Bacchus' votaries, he drove
With brandish'd steel from Nyssa's sacred grove ;
Their consecrated spears lay scatter'd round,   165
With curling vines and twisted ivy bound ;
While Bacchus headlong sought the briny flood,

And Thetis' arms received the trembling god.
Nor fail'd the crime th' immortals' wrath to move,
(Th' immortals bless'd with endless ease above;)   170
Depriv'd of sight, by their avenging doom,
Cheerless he breath'd, and wander'd in the gloom :
Then sunk unpitied to the dire abodes,
A wretch accurs'd, and hated by the gods !
I brave not heaven ; but if the fruits of earth   175
Sustain thy life, and human be thy birth,
Bold as thou art, too prodigal of breath,
Approach, and enter the dark gates of death."
   " What, or from whence I am, or who my sire,"
(Replied the chief,) " can Tydeus' son inquire?   180
Like leaves on trees the race of man is found,
Now green in youth, now withering on the ground :
Another race the following spring supplies,
They fall successive, and successive rise ;
So generations in their course decay,   185
So flourish these, when those are past away.
But if thou still persist to search my birth,
Then hear a tale that fills the spacious earth :
   " A city stands on Argos' utmost bound ;
(Argos the fair, for warlike steeds renown'd ;)   190
Æolian Sisyphus, with wisdom bless'd,
In ancient time the happy walls possess'd,
Then call'd Ephyré : Glaucus was his son ;
Great Glaucus, father of Bellerophon,
Who o'er the sons of men in beauty shin'd,   195
Lov'd for that valour which preserves mankind.
Then mighty Prœtus Argos' sceptre sway'd,
Whose hard commands Bellerophon obey'd.

D

With direful jealousy the monarch raged,
And the brave prince in numerous toils engaged.   200
For him, Antea burn'd with lawless flame,
And strove to tempt him from the paths of fame :
In vain she tempted the relentless youth,
Endued with wisdom, sacred fear, and truth.
Fir'd at his scorn, the queen to Prœtus fled,   205
And begg'd revenge for her insulted bed :
Incens'd he heard, resolving on his fate ;
But hospitable laws restrain'd his hate :
To Lycia the devoted youth he sent,
With tablets-seal'd, that told his dire intent.   210
Now, bless'd by every power who guards the good,
The chief arriv'd at Xanthus' silver flood :
There Lycia's monarch paid him honours due ;
Nine days he feasted, and nine bulls he slew.
But when the tenth bright morning orient glow'd,   215
The faithful youth his monarch's mandate show'd :
The fatal tablets, till that instant seal'd,
The deathful secret to the king reveal'd.
First, dire Chimæra's conquest was enjoin'd ;
A mingled monster, of no mortal kind ;   220
Behind, a dragon's fiery tail was spread ;
A goat's rough body bore a lion's head ;
Her pitchy nostrils flaky flames expire ;
Her gaping throat emits infernal fire.
  "This pest he slaughter'd ; (for he read the skies,   225
And trusted heaven's informing prodigies ;)
Then met in arms the Solymæan crew,
(Fiercest of men,) and those the warrior slew.
Next the bold Amazons' whole force defied ;

And conquer'd still, for heaven was on his side.   230
   " Nor ended here his toils : his Lycian foes,
At his return, a treacherous ambush rose,
With levell'd spears along the winding shore :
There fell they breathless, and return'd no more.
   " At length the monarch with repentant grief   235
Confess'd the gods, and god-descended chief ;
His daughter gave, the stranger to detain,
With half the honours of his ample reign.
The Lycians grant a chosen space of ground,
With woods, with vineyards, and with harvests crown'd. 240
There long the chief his happy lot possess'd,
With two brave sons and one fair daughter bless'd :
(Fair e'en in heavenly eyes ; her fruitful love
Crown'd with Sarpedon's birth th' embrace of Jove.)
But when at last, distracted in his mind,   245
Forsook by heaven, forsaking human kind,
Wide o'er th' Aleian field he chose to stray,
A long, forlorn, uncomfortable way !
Woes heap'd on woes consum'd his wasted heart ;
His beauteous daughter fell by Phœbe's dart ;   250
His eldest-born by raging Mars was slain,
In combat on the Solymæan plain.
Hippolochus surviv'd ; from him I came,
The honour'd author of my birth and name ;
By his decree I sought the Trojan town,   255
By his instructions learn to win renown ;
To stand the first in worth as in command,
To add new honours to my native land ;
Before my eyes my mighty sires to place,
And emulate the glories of our race."   260

He spoke, and transport fill'd Tydides' heart;
In earth the generous warrior fix'd his dart,
Then friendly, thus, the Lycian prince address'd:
" Welcome, my brave hereditary guest!
Thus ever let us meet with kind embrace,   265
Nor stain the sacred friendship of our race.
Know, chief, our grandsires have been guests of old,
Œneus the strong, Bellerophon the bold;
Our ancient seat his honour'd presence graced,
Where twenty days in genial rites he pass'd.   270
The parting heroes mutual presents left;
A golden goblet was thy grandsire's gift;
Œneus a belt of matchless work bestow'd,
That rich with Tyrian dye refulgent glow'd.
(This from his pledge I learn'd, which, safely stor'd   275
Among my treasures, still adorns my board:
For Tydeus left me young when Thebé's wall
Beheld the sons of Greece untimely fall.)
Mindful of this, in friendship let us join;
If heaven our steps to foreign lands incline,   280
My guest in Argos thou, and I in Lycia thine.
Enough of Trojans to this lance shall yield,
In the full harvest of yon ample field;
Enough of Greeks shall dye thy spear with gore;
But thou and Diomed be foes no more.   285
Now change we arms, and prove to either host
We guard the friendship of the line we boast."
    Thus having said, the gallant chiefs alight,
Their hands they join, their mutual faith they plight;
Brave Glaucus then each narrow thought resign'd;   290
(Jove warm'd his bosom and enlarged his mind;)

For Diomed's brass arms, of mean device,
For which nine oxen paid, (a vulgar price,)
He gave his own, of gold divinely wrought ;
A hundred beeves the shining purchase bought.   295
   Meantime the guardian of the Trojan state,
Great Hector, enter'd at the Scæan gate.
Beneath the beech-trees' consecrated shades,
The Trojan matrons and the Trojan maids
Around him flock'd, all press'd with pious care   300
For husbands, brothers, sons, engaged in war.
He bids the train in long procession go,
And seek the gods, t' avert th' impending woe.
And now to Priam's stately courts he came,
Rais'd on arch'd columns of stupendous frame ;   305
O'er these a range of marble structure runs ;
The rich pavilions of his fifty sons,
In fifty chambers lodged : and rooms of state
Oppos'd to those, where Priam's daughters sate :
Twelve domes for them and their lov'd spouses shone,   310
Of equal beauty, and of polish'd stone.
Hither great Hector pass'd, nor pass'd unseen
Of royal Hecuba, his mother queen.
(With her Laodicé, whose beauteous face
Surpass'd the nymphs of Troy's illustrious race.)   315
Long in a strict embrace she held her son,
And press'd his hand, and tender thus begun :
   " O Hector ! say, what great occasion calls
My son from fight, when Greece surrounds our walls ?
Com'st thou to supplicate th' almighty power   320
With lifted hands from Ilion's lofty tower ?
Stay, till I bring the cup with Bacchus crown'd,

In Jove's high name, to sprinkle on the ground,
And pay due vows to all the gods around.
Then with a plenteous draught refresh thy soul,   325
And draw new spirits from the generous bowl;
Spent as thou art with long laborious fight,
The brave defender of thy country's right."
　　" Far hence be Bacchus' gifts;" (the chief rejoin'd;)
" Inflaming wine, pernicious to mankind,   330
Unnerves the limbs and dulls the noble mind.
Let chiefs abstain, and spare the sacred juice
To sprinkle to the gods, its better use.
By me that holy office were profan'd;
Ill fits it me, with human gore distain'd,   335
To the pure skies these horrid hands to raise,
Or offer heaven's great sire polluted praise.
You, with your matrons, go, a spotless train!
And burn rich odours in Minerva's fane.
The largest mantle your full wardrobes hold,   340
Most priz'd for art, and labour'd o'er with gold,
Before the goddess' honour'd knees be spread,
And twelve young heifers to her altar led.
So may the power, aton'd by fervent prayer,
Our wives, our infants, and our city spare,   . 345
And far avert Tydides' wasteful ire,
Who mows whole troops, and makes all Troy retire.
Be this, O mother, your religious care;
I go to rouse soft Paris to the war;
If yet, not lost to all the sense of shame,   350
The recreant warrior hear the voice of fame.
Oh would kind earth the hateful wretch embrace,
That pest of Troy, that ruin of our race!

Deep to the dark abyss might he descend,
Troy yet should flourish, and my sorrows end."   355
    This heard, she gave command ; and summon'd came
Each noble matron, and illustrious dame.
The Phrygian queen to her rich wardrobe went,
Where treasur'd odours breath'd a costly scent.
There lay the vestures of no vulgar art,   360
Sidonian maids embroider'd every part,
Whom from soft Sidon youthful Paris bore,
With Helen touching on the Tyrian shore.
Here as the queen revolv'd with careful eyes
The various textures and the various dyes,   365
She chose a veil that shone superior far,
And glow'd refulgent as the morning star.
Herself with this the long procession leads ;
The train majestically slow proceeds.
Soon as to Ilion's topmost tower they come,   370
And awful reach the high Palladian dome,
Antenor's consort, fair Theano, waits
As Pallas' priestess, and unbars the gates.
With hands uplifted and imploring eyes,
They fill the dome with supplicating cries.   375
The priestess then the shining veil displays,
Placed on Minerva's knees and thus she prays :
    "Oh, awful goddess ! ever-dreadful maid,
Troy's strong defence, unconquer'd Pallas, aid !
Break thou Tydides' spear, and let him fall   380
Prone on the dust before the Trojan wall.
So twelve young heifers, guiltless of the yoke,
Shall fill thy temple with a grateful smoke.
But thou, aton'd by penitence and prayer,

Ourselves, our infants, and our city spare !" 385
So pray'd the priestess in her holy fane ;
So vow'd the matrons, but they vow'd in vain.
　While these appear before the power with prayers,
Hector to Paris' lofty dome repairs.
Himself the mansion rais'd, from every part 390
Assembling architects of matchless art.
Near Priam's court and Hector's palace stands
The pompous structure, and the town commands.
A spear the hero bore of wondrous strength,
Of full ten cubits was the lance's length ; 395
The steely point with golden ringlets join'd,
Before him brandish'd at each motion shin'd.
Thus entering, in the glittering rooms he found
His brother-chief, whose useless arms lay round,
His eyes delighting with their splendid show 400
Bright'ning the shield, and polishing the bow.
Beside him Helen with her virgins stands,
Guides their rich labours, and instructs their hands.
　Him thus inactive, with an ardent look
The prince beheld, and high-resenting spoke : 405
"Thy hate to Troy is this the time to shew ?
(Oh wretch ill-fated, and thy country's foe !)
Paris and Greece against us both conspire,
Thy close resentment, and their vengeful ire.
For thee great Ilion's guardian heroes fall, 410
Till heaps of dead alone defend her wall ;
For thee the soldier bleeds, the matron mourns,
And wasteful war in all its fury burns.
Ungrateful man ! deserves not this thy care,
Our troops to hearten, and our toils to share ? 415

Rise, or behold the conquering flames ascend,
And all the Phrygian glories at an end."
    " Brother, 'tis just," (replied the beauteous youth,)
"Thy free remonstrance proves thy worth and truth :
Yet charge my absence less, oh generous chief !   420
On hate to Troy, than conscious shame and grief.
Here, hid from human eyes, thy brother sat,
And mourn'd in secret his and Ilion's fate.
'Tis now enough : now glory spreads her charms,
And beauteous Helen calls her chief to arms.   425
Conquest to-day my happier sword may bless,
'Tis man's to fight, but heaven's to give success.
But while I arm, contain thy ardent mind ;
Or go, and Paris shall not lag behind."
    He said, nor answer'd Priam's warlike son ;   430
When Helen thus with lowly grace begun :
    " Oh generous brother ! if the guilty dame
That caus'd these woes deserves a sister's name !
Would heaven, ere all these dreadful deeds were done,
The day that show'd me to the golden sun   435
Had seen my death !   Why did not whirlwinds bear
The fatal infant to the fowls of air?
Why sunk I not beneath the whelming tide,
And midst the roaring of the waters died?
Heaven fill'd up all my ills, and I accurs'd   440
Bore all, and Paris of those ills the worst.
Helen at least a braver spouse might claim,
Warm'd with some virtue, some regard of fame !
Now, tired with toils, thy fainting limbs recline,
With toils sustain'd for Paris' sake and mine :   445
The gods have link'd our miserable doom,

Our present woe and infamy to come ;
Wide shall it spread, and last through ages long,
Example sad ! and theme of future song."

    The chief replied : " This time forbids to rest :   450
The Trojan bands, by hostile fury press'd,
Demand their Hector, and his arm require ;
The combat urges, and my soul's on fire.
Urge thou thy knight to march where glory calls,
And timely join me, ere I leave the walls.   455
Ere yet I mingle in the direful fray,
My wife, my infant, claim a moment's stay :
This day (perhaps the last that sees me here)
Demands a parting word, a tender tear :
This day some god, who hates our Trojan land,   460
May vanquish Hector by a Grecian hand."

    He said, and pass'd with sad presaging heart
To seek his spouse, his soul's far dearei part ;
At home he sought her, but he sought in vain :
She, with one maid of all her menial train,   465
Had thence retir'd ; and, with her second joy,
The young Astyanax, the hope of Troy,
Pensive she stood on Ilion's tow'ry height,
Beheld the war, and sicken'd at the sight ;
There her sad eyes in vain her lord explore,   470
Or weep the wounds her bleeding country bore.

    But he who found not whom his soul desir'd,
Whose virtue charm'd him as her beauty fir'd,
Stood in the gates, and ask'd what way she bent   475
Her parting steps?   If to the fane she went,
Where late the mourning matrons made resort ;
Or sought her sisters in the Trojan court?

"Not to the court," (replied th' attendant train,)
"Nor, mix'd with matrons, to Minerva's fane:
To Ilion's steepy tower she bent her way,   480
To mark the fortunes of the doubtful day.
Troy fled, she heard, before the Grecian sword:
She heard, and trembled for her distant lord;
Distracted with surprise, she seem'd to fly,
Fear on her cheek, and sorrow in her eye.   485
The nurse attended, with her infant boy,
The young Astyanax, the hope of Troy."
    Hector, this heard, return'd without delay;
Swift through the town he trod his former way,
Through streets of palaces and walks of state;   490
And met the mourner at the Scæan gate.
With haste to meet him sprung the joyful fair,
His blameless wife, Eëtion's wealthy heir:
(Cilician Thebé great Eëtion sway'd,
And Hippoplacus' wide-extended shade:)   495
The nurse stood near, in whose embraces press'd,
His only hope hung smiling at her breast,
Whom each soft charm and early grace adorn,
Fair as the new-born star that gilds the morn.
To this lov'd infant Hector gave the name   500
Scamandrius, from Scamander's honour'd stream:
Astyanax the Trojans call'd the boy,
From his great father, the defence of Troy.
Silent the warrior smil'd, and pleas'd, resign'd
To tender passions all his mighty mind: 505
His beauteous princess cast a mournful look,
Hung on his hand, and then dejected spoke;
Her bosom labour'd with a boding sigh,

And the big tear stood trembling in her eye.
   "Too daring prince ! ah whither dost thou run ?   510
Ah too forgetful of thy wife and son !
And think'st thou not how wretched we shall be,
A widow I, a helpless orphan he !
For sure such courage, length of life denies,
And thou must fall, thy virtue's sacrifice.   515
Greece in her single heroes strove in vain ;
Now hosts oppose thee, and thou must be slain !
Oh grant me, gods ! ere Hector meets his doom,
All I can ask of heaven, an early tomb !
So shall my days in one sad tenor run,   520
And end with sorrows as they first begun.
No parent now remains, my griefs to share,
No father's aid, no mother's tender care.
The fierce Achilles wrapt our walls in fire,
Laid Thebé waste, and slew my warlike sire !   525
His fate compassion in the victor bred ;
Stern as he was, he yet rever'd the dead,
His radiant arms preserv'd from hostile spoil,
And laid him decent on the funeral pile ;
Then rais'd a mountain where his bones were burn'd ; 530
The mountain nymphs the rural tomb adorn'd ;
Jove's sylvan daughters bade their elms bestow
A barren shade, and in his honour grow.
   " By the same arm my seven brave brothers fell ;
In one sad day beheld the gates of hell ;   535
While the fat herds and snowy flocks they fed,
Amid their fields the hapless heroes bled !
My mother liv'd to bear the victor's bands,
The queen of Hippoplacia's sylvan lands :

Redeem'd too late, she scarce beheld again   540
Her pleasing empire and her native plain,
When, ah ! oppress'd by life-consuming woe,
She fell a victim to Diana's bow.
  "Yet while my Hector still survives, I see
My father, mother, brethren, all, in thee.   545
Alas ! my parents, brothers, kindred, all
Once more will perish if my Hector fall.
Thy wife, thy infant, in thy danger share ;
Oh prove a husband's and a father's care !
That quarter most the skilful Greeks annoy   550
Where yon wild fig-trees join the wall of Troy :
Thou, from this tower defend th' important post ;
There Agamemnon points his dreadful host,
That pass Tydides, Ajax, strive to gain,
And there the vengeful Spartan fires his train.   555
Thrice our bold foes the fierce attack have given,
Or led by hopes, or dictated from heaven.
Let others in the field their arms employ,
But stay my Hector here, and guard his Troy."
  The chief replied : "That post shall be my care, 560
Nor that alone, but all the works of war.
How would the sons of Troy, in arms renown'd,
And Troy's proud dames, whose garments sweep the
     ground,
Attaint the lustre of my former name,
Should Hector basely quit the field of fame?   565
My early youth was bred to martial pains,
My soul impels me to th' embattled plains :
Let me be foremost to defend the throne,
And guard my father's glories, and my own.

Yet come it will, the day decreed by fates ;   570
(How my heart trembles while my tongue relates !)
The day when thou, imperial Troy ! must bend,
And see thy warriors fall, thy glories end.
And yet no dire presage so wounds my mind,
My mother's death, the ruin of my kind,   575
Not Priam's hoary hairs defil'd with gore,
Not all my brothers gasping on the shore ;
As thine, Andromache ! thy griefs I dread ;
I see thee trembling, weeping, captive led !
In Argive looms our battles to design,   580
And woes of which so large a part was thine !
To bear the victor's hard commands, or bring
The weight of waters from Hyperia's spring.
There, while you groan beneath the load of life,
They cry, Behold the mighty Hector's wife !   585
Some haughty Greek, who lives thy tears to see,
Embitters all thy woes by naming me.
The thoughts of glory past, and present shame,
A thousand griefs, shall waken at the name !
May I lie cold before that dreadful day,   590
Press'd with a load of monumental clay !
Thy Hector, wrapp'd in everlasting sleep,
Shall neither hear thee sigh, nor see thee weep."
   Thus having spoke, th' illustrious chief of Troy
Stretch'd his fond arms to clasp the lovely boy.   595
The babe clung crying to his nurse's breast,
Scar'd at the dazzling helm, and nodding crest.
With secret pleasure each fond parent smil'd,
And Hector hasted to relieve his child ;
The glittering terrors from his brows unbound,   600

Friedrich Preller.

ILIAD — BOOK VI., 488–615.

And placed the beaming helmet on the ground.
Then kiss'd the child, and, lifting high in air,
Thus to the gods preferr'd a father's prayer:
"O thou ! whose glory fills th' ethereal throne,
And all ye deathless powers ! protect my son !   605
Grant him, like me, to purchase just renown,
To guard the Trojans, to defend the crown,
Against his country's foes the war to wage,
And rise the Hector of the future age !
So when, triumphant from successful toils,   610
Of heroes slain he bears the reeking spoils,
Whole hosts may hail him with deserv'd acclaim,
And say, This chief transcends his father's fame :
While pleas'd, amidst the general shouts of Troy,
His mother's conscious heart o'erflows with joy."   615
    He spoke, and fondly gazing on her charms
Restor'd the pleasing burden to her arms ;
Soft on her fragrant breast the babe she laid,
Hush'd to repose, and with a smile survey'd.
The troubled pleasure soon chastis'd by fear,   620
She mingled with the smile a tender tear.
The soften'd chief with kind compassion view'd,
And dried the falling drops, and thus pursued :
    " Andromache ! my soul's far better part,
Why with untimely sorrows heaves thy heart?   625
No hostile hand can antedate my doom,
Till fate condemns me to the silent tomb.
Fix'd is the term to all the race of earth,
And such the hard condition of our birth.
No force can then resist, no flight can save ;   630
All sink alike, the fearful and the brave.

No more — but hasten to thy tasks at home,
There guide the spindle, and direct the loom :
Me glory summons to the martial scene,
The field of combat is the sphere for men.   635
Where heroes war, the foremost place I claim,
The first in danger as the first in fame."

 Thus having said, the glorious chief resumes
His towery helmet, black with shading plumes.
His princess parts with a prophetic sigh,   640
Unwilling parts, and oft reverts her eye,
That stream'd at every look : then, moving slow,
Sought her own palace, and indulged her woe.
There, while her tears deplored the godlike man,
Through all her train the soft infection ran ;   645
The pious maids their mingled sorrows shed,
And mourn the living Hector as the dead.

 But now, no longer deaf to honour's call,
Forth issues Paris from the palace wall.
In brazen arms that cast a gleamy ray,   650
Swift through the town the warrior bends his way.
The wanton courser thus, with reins unbound,
Breaks from his stall, and beats the trembling ground ;
Pamper'd and proud he seeks the wonted tides,
And laves, in height of blood, his shining sides :   655
His head now freed he tosses to the skies ;
His mane dishevell'd o'er his shoulders flies ;
He snuffs the females in the distant.plain,
And springs, exulting, to his fields again.
With equal triumph, sprightly, bold and gay,   660
In arms refulgent as the god of day,
The son of Priam, glorying in his might,

Rush'd forth with Hector to the fields of fight.
   And now the warriors passing on the way,
The graceful Paris first excused his stay.   665
To whom the noble Hector thus replied :
" O chief ! in blood, and now in arms, allied !
Thy power in war with justice none contest ;
Known is thy courage, and thy strength confess'd.
What pity, sloth should seize a soul so brave,   670
Or godlike Paris live a woman's slave !
My heart weeps blood at what the Trojans say,
And hopes thy deeds shall wipe the stain away.
Haste then, in all their glorious labours share ;
For much they suffer, for thy sake, in war.   675
These ills shall cease, whene'er by Jove's decree
We crown the bowl to Heaven and Liberty :
While the proud foe his frustrate triumphs mourns,
And Greece indignant through her seas returns."

   E

J. Flaxman and A. Schill.

BOOK XXII.

THE DEATH OF HECTOR.

Thus to their bulwarks, smit with panic fear,
The herded Ilians rush like driven deer;
There safe, they wipe the briny drops away,
And drown in bowls the labours of the day.
Close to the walls, advancing o'er the fields,   5
Beneath one roof of well-compacted shields,
March, bending on, the Greeks' embodied powers,
Far-stretching in the shade of Trojan towers.
Great Hector singly stay'd; chain'd down by fate,
There fix'd he stood before the Scæan gate;   10
Still his bold arms determin'd to employ,
The guardian still of long-defended Troy.
    Apollo now to tir'd Achilles turns,
(The power confess'd in all his glory burns,)

"And what" (he cries) "has Peleus' son in view,   15
With mortal speed a godhead to pursue?
For not to thee to know the gods is giv'n,
Unskill'd to trace the latent marks of heav'n.
What boots thee now, that Troy forsook the plain?
Vain thy past labour, and thy present vain :   20
Safe in their walls are now her troops bestow'd,
While here thy frantic rage attacks a god."
    The chief incens'd : "Too partial god of day !
To check my conquests in the middle way :
How few in Ilion else had refuge found !   25
What gasping numbers now had bit the ground !
Thou robb'st me of a glory justly mine,
Powerful of godhead, and of fraud divine :
Mean fame, alas ! for one of heavenly strain,
To cheat a mortal who repines in vain."   30
    Then to the city, terrible and strong,
With high and haughty steps he tower'd along :
So the proud courser, victor of the prize,
To the near goal with double ardour flies.
Him, as he blazing shot across the field,   35
The careful eyes of Priam first beheld.
Not half so dreadful rises to the sight,
Through the thick gloom of some tempestuous night,
Orion's dog, (the year when autumn weighs,)
And o'er the feebler stars exerts his rays ;   40
Terrific glory ! for his burning breath
Taints the red air with fevers, plagues, and death.
So flam'd his fiery mail.   Then wept the sage :
He strikes his rev'rend head, now white with age ;
He lifts his wither'd arms ; obtests the skies ;   45

He calls his much-lov'd son with feeble cries :
The son, resolv'd Achilles' force to dare,
Full at the Scæan gate expects the war :
While the sad father on the rampart stands,
And thus adjures him with extended hands :   50
  " Ah stay not, stay not ! guardless and alone ;
Hector, my lov'd, my dearest, bravest son !
Methinks already I behold thee slain,
And stretch'd beneath that fury of the plain.
Implacable Achilles ! might'st thou be   55
To all the gods no dearer than to me !
Thee vultures wild should scatter round the shore,
And bloody dogs grow fiercer from thy gore !
How many valiant sons I late enjoy'd,
Valiant in vain ! by thy curs'd arm destroy'd :   60
Or, worse than slaughter'd, sold in distant isles
To shameful bondage and unworthy toils.
Two, while I speak, my eyes in vain explore,
Two from one mother sprung, my Polydore
And loved Lycaon ; now perhaps no more !   65
Oh ! if in yonder hostile camp they live,
What heaps of gold, what treasures would I give !
(Their grandsire's wealth, by right of birth their own,
Consign'd his daughter with Lelegia's throne :)
But if (which heaven forbid) already lost,   70
All pale they wander on the Stygian coast,
What sorrows then must their sad mother know,
What anguish I ! unutterable woe !
Yet less that anguish, less to her, to me,
Less to all Troy, if not deprived of thee.   75
Yet shun Achilles ! enter yet the wall ;

And spare thyself, thy father, spare us all !
Save thy dear life : or if a soul so brave
Neglect that thought, thy dearer glory save.
Pity, while yet I live, these silver hairs ;   80
While yet thy father feels the woes he bears,
Yet curs'd with sense ! a wretch, whom in his rage
(All trembling on the verge of helpless age)
Great Jove has placed, sad spectacle of pain !
The bitter dregs of fortune's cup to drain :   85
To fill with scenes of death his closing eyes,
And number all his days by miseries !
My heroes slain, my bridal bed o'erturned,
My daughters ravish'd, and my city burn'd,
My bleeding infants dash'd against the floor ;   90
These I have yet to see, perhaps yet more !
Perhaps ev'n I, reserv'd by angry fate
The last sad relic of my ruined state,
(Dire pomp of sovereign wretchedness !) must fall
And stain the pavement of my regal hall ;   95
Where famish'd dogs, late guardians of my door,
Shall lick their mangled master's spatter'd gore.
Yet for my sons I thank ye, gods ! 'twas well :
Well have they perish'd, for in fight they fell.
Who dies in youth and vigour, dies the best,   100
Struck through with wounds, all honest on the breast.
But when the fates, in fulness of their rage,
Spurn the hoar head of unresisting age,
In dust the reverend lineaments deform,
And pour to dogs the life-blood scarcely warm ;   105
This, this is misery ! the last, the worst,
That man can feel : man, fated to be curs'.

He said, and acting what no words could say,
Rent from his head the silver locks away.
With him the mournful mother bears a part:　　110
Yet all their sorrows turn not Hector's heart:
The zone unbraced, her bosom she display'd;
And thus, fast-falling the salt tears, she said:
　　" Have mercy on me, O my son ! revere
The words of age ; attend a parent's prayer !　　115
If ever thee in these fond arms I press'd,
Or still'd thy infant clamours at this breast ;
Ah ! do not thus our helpless years forego,
But, by our walls secured, repel the foe.
Against his rage if singly thou proceed,　　120
Should'st thou, (but heav'n avert it !) should'st thou
　　bleed,
Nor must thy corse lie honour'd on the bier,
Nor spouse, nor mother, grace thee with a tear ;
Far from our pious rites, those dear remains
Must feast the vultures on the naked plains."　　125
　　So they, while down their cheeks the torrents roll :
But fix'd remains the purpose of his soul ;
Resolv'd he stands, and with a fiery glance
Expects the hero's terrible advance.
So, roll'd up in his den, the swelling snake　　130
Beholds the traveller approach the brake ;
When, fed with noxious herbs, his turgid veins
Have gather'd half the poisons of the plains ;
He burns, he stiffens with collected ire,
And his red eyeballs glare with living fire.　　135
Beneath a turret, on his shield reclin'd,
He stood, and question'd thus his mighty mind :

"Where lies my way? To enter in the wall?
Honour and shame th' ungenerous thought recall:
Shall proud Polydamas before the gate   140
Proclaim, his counsels are obey'd too late,
Which timely follow'd but the former night,
What numbers had been sav'd by Hector's flight?
That wise advice rejected with disdain,
I feel my folly in my people slain.   145
Methinks my suffering country's voice I hear,
But most, her worthless sons insult my ear,
On my rash courage charge the chance of war,
And blame those virtues which they cannot share.
No — If I e'er return, return I must   150
Glorious, my country's terror laid in dust:
Or if I perish, let her see me fall
In field at least, and fighting for her wall.
And yet suppose these measures I forego,
Approach unarm'd, and parley with the foe,   155
The warrior-shield, the helm, and lance lay down,
And treat on terms of peace to save the town:
The wife withheld, the treasure ill-detain'd,
(Cause of the war, and grievance of the land,)
With honourable justice to restore;   160
And add half Ilion's yet remaining store,
Which Troy shall, sworn, produce; that injur'd Greece
May share our wealth, and leave our walls in peace.
But why this thought? unarm'd if I should go,
What hope of mercy from this vengeful foe,   165
But woman-like to fall, and fall without a blow?
We greet not here, as man conversing man,
Met at an oak, or journeying o'er a plain;

No season now for calm, familiar talk,
Like youths and maidens in an ev'ning walk :   170
War is our business, but to whom is given
To die or triumph, that determine heaven !"
　　Thus pondering, like a god the Greek drew nigh :
His dreadful plumage nodded from on high ;
The Pelian javelin, in his better hand,   175
Shot trembling rays that glitter'd o'er the land ;
And on his breast the beamy splendours shone
Like Jove's own lightning, or the rising sun.
As Hector sees, unusual terrors rise,
Struck by some god, he fears, recedes, and flies :   180
He leaves the gates, he leaves the walls behind ;
Achilles follows like the wingèd wind.
Thus at the panting dove the falcon flies ;
(The swiftest racer of the liquid skies ;)
Just when he holds, or thinks he holds, his prey,   185
Obliquely wheeling through th' aërial way,
With open beak and shrilling cries he springs
And aims his claws, and shoots upon his wings :
No less fore-right the rapid chase they held,
One urged by fury, one by fear impell'd ;   190
Now circling round the walls their course maintain,
Where the high watch-tower overlooks the plain ;
Now where the fig-trees spread their umbrage broad,
(A wider compass,) smoke along the road.
Next by Scamander's double source they bound,   195
Where two fam'd fountains burst the parted ground :
This hot through scorching clefts is seen to rise,
With exhalations steaming to the skies ;
That the green banks in summer's heat o'erflows,

Like crystal clear, and cold as winter snows.   200
Each gushing fount a marble cistern fills,
Whose polish'd bed receives the falling rills;
Where Trojan dames (ere yet alarm'd by Greece)
Wash'd their fair garments in the days of peace.
By these they pass'd, one chasing, one in flight;   205
(The mighty fled, pursued by stronger might;)
Swift was the course; no vulgar prize they play,
No vulgar victim must reward the day;
(Such as in races crown the speedy strife;)
The prize contended was great Hector's life.   210
    As when some hero's funerals are decreed,
In grateful honour of the mighty dead;
Where high rewards the vigorous youth inflame,
(Some golden tripod, or some lovely dame,)
The panting coursers swiftly turn the goal,   215
And with them turns the rais'd spectator's soul:
Thus three times round the Trojan wall they fly;
The gazing gods lean forward from the sky:
To whom, while eager on the chase they look,
The sire of mortals and immortals spoke: 220
    "Unworthy sight! the man, belov'd of heaven,
Behold, inglorious round yon city driven!
My heart partakes the generous Hector's pain;
Hector, whose zeal whole hecatombs has slain.
Whose grateful fumes the gods receiv'd with joy,   225
From Ida's summits, and the towers of Troy:
Now see him flying! to his fears resign'd,
And Fate, and fierce Achilles, close behind.
Consult, ye powers ('tis worthy your debate),
Whether to snatch him from impending fate,   230

Or let him bear, by stern Pelides slain,
(Good as he is,) the lot impos'd on man?"
 Then Pallas thus: "Shall he whose vengeance forms
The forky bolt, and blackens heaven with storms,
Shall he prolong one Trojan's forfeit breath,   235
A man, a mortal, pre-ordain'd to death?
And will no murmurs fill the courts above?
No gods indignant blame their partial Jove?"
"Go then," (return'd the sire,) "without delay;
Exert thy will: I give the fates their way."   240
Swift at the mandate pleas'd Tritonia flies,
And stoops impetuous from the cleaving skies.
 As through the forest, o'er the vale and lawn,
The well-breath'd beagle drives the flying fawn;
In vain he tries the covert of the brakes,   245
Or deep beneath the trembling thicket shakes:
Sure of the vapour in the tainted dews,
The certain hound his various maze pursues:
Thus step by step, where'er the Trojan wheel'd,
There swift Achilles compass'd round the field.   250
Oft as to reach the Dardan gates he bends,
And hopes th' assistance of his pitying friends,
(Whose showering arrows, as he cours'd below,
From the high turrets might oppress the foe,)
So oft Achilles turns him to the plain: 255
He eyes the city, but he eyes in vain.
As men in slumber seem with speedy pace,
One to pursue, and one to lead the chase,
Their sinking limbs the fancied course forsake.
Nor this can fly, nor that can overtake: 260
No less the lab'ring heroes pant and strain;

While that but flies, and this pursues, in vain.
    What god, O Muse ! assisted Hector's force,
With Fate itself so long to hold the course ?
Phœbus it was : who, in his latest hour,   265
Endued his knees with strength, his nerves with power.
And great Achilles, lest some Greek's advance
Should snatch the glory from his lifted lance,
Sign'd to the troops, to yield his foe the way,
And leave untouch'd the honours of the day.   270
    Jove lifts the golden balances, that show
The fates of mortal men, and things below :
Here each contending hero's lot he tries,
And weighs, with equal hand, their destinies.
Low sinks the scale surcharged with Hector's fate ;   275
Heavy with death it sinks, and hell receives the weight.
    Then Phœbus left him.   Fierce Minerva flies
To stern Pelides, and, triumphing, cries :
" Oh lov'd of Jove ! this day our labours cease,
And conquest blazes with full beams on Greece.   280
Great Hector falls ; that Hector fam'd so far,
Drunk with renown, insatiable of war,
Falls by thy hand, and mine ! nor force nor flight
Shall more avail him, nor his god of light.
See, where in vain he supplicates above,   285
Roll'd at the feet of unrelenting Jove !
Rest here : myself will lead the Trojan on,
And urge to meet the fate he cannot shun."
    Her voice divine the chief with joyful mind
Obey'd, and rested, on his lance reclined.   290
While like Deïphobus the martial dame,
(Her face, her gesture, and her arms, the same,)

In show an aid, by hapless Hector's side
Approach'd, and greets him thus with voice belied:
    "Too long, O Hector! have I born the sight   295
Of this distress, and sorrow'd in thy flight:
It fits us now a noble stand to make,   -
And here, as brothers, equal fates partake."
    Then he: "O prince! allied in blood and fame,
Dearer than all that own a brother's name;   300
Of all that Hecuba to Priam bore,
Long tried, long lov'd; much lov'd, but honour'd more!
Since you of all our numerous race alone
Defend my life, regardless of your own."
    Again the goddess: "Much my father's prayer,   305
And much my mother's, press'd me to forbear:
My friends embraced my knees, adjur'd my stay,
But stronger love impell'd, and I obey.
Come then, the glorious conflict let us try,
Let the steel sparkle and the javelin fly;   310
Or let us stretch Achilles on the field,
Or to his arm our bloody trophies yield."
    Fraudful she said; then swiftly march'd before;
The Dardan hero shuns his foe no more.
Sternly they met.   The silence Hector broke;   315
His dreadful plumage nodded as he spoke:
    "Enough, O son of Peleus! Troy has view'd
Her walls thrice circled, and her chief pursu'd.
But now some god within me bids me try
Thine, or my fate: I kill thee, or I die.   320
Yet on the verge of battle let us stay,
And for a moment's space suspend the day:
Let heaven's high powers be call'd to arbitrate

The just conditions of this stern debate :
(Eternal witnesses of all below, 325
And faithful guardians of the treasur'd vow !)
To them I swear : if, victor in the strife,
Jove by these hands shall shed thy noble life,
No vile dishonour shall thy corse pursue ;
Stripp'd of its arms alone, (the conqueror's due,) 330
The rest to Greece uninjur'd I'll restore :
Now plight thy mutual oath, I ask no more."
　"Talk not of oaths," (the dreadful chief replies,
While anger flash'd from his disdainful eyes,)
" Detested as thou art, and ought to be, 335
Nor oath nor pact Achilles plights with thee ;
Such pacts, as lambs and rabid wolves combine,
Such leagues, as men and furious lions join,
To such I call the gods ! one constant state
Of lasting rancour and eternal hate : 340
No thought but rage, and never-ceasing strife,
Till death extinguish rage, and thought, and life.
Rouse then thy forces this important hour,
Collect thy soul, and call forth all thy power.
No farther subterfuge, no farther chance ; 345
' Tis Pallas, Pallas gives thee to my lance.
Each Grecian ghost by thee deprived of breath,
Now hovers round, and calls thee to thy death."
　He spoke, and launch'd his javelin at the foe ;
But Hector shunn'd the meditated blow : 350
He stoop'd, while o'er his head the flying spear
Sung innocent, and spent its force in air.
Minerva watch'd it falling on the land,
Then drew, and gave to great Achilles' hand,

Unseen of Hector, who elate with joy,   355
Now shakes his lance, and braves the dread of Troy:
  "The life you boasted to that javelin given,
Prince ! you have miss'd. My fate depends on heaven.
To thee (presumptuous as thou art) unknown
Or what must prove my fortune, or thy own.   360
Boasting is but an art, our fears to blind,
And with false terrors sink another's mind.
But know, whatever fate I am to try,
By no dishonest wound shall Hector die ;
I shall not fall a fugitive at least,   365
My soul shall bravely issue from my breast.
But first, try thou my arm ; and may this dart
End all my country's woes, deep buried in thy heart !"
  The weapon flew, its course unerring held ;
Unerring, but the heavenly shield repell'd   370
The mortal dart ; resulting with a bound
From off the ringing orb, it struck the ground.
Hector beheld his javelin fall in vain, -
Nor other lance nor other hope remain ;
He calls Deïphobus, demands a spear,   375
In vain, for no Deïphobus was there.
All comfortless he stands : then, with a sigh,
  " 'Tis so — heaven wills it, and my hour is nigh!
I deem'd Deïphobus had heard my call,
But he secure lies guarded in the wall.   380
A god deceiv'd me ; Pallas, 'twas thy deed :
Death and black fate approach ! 'tis I must bleed :
No refuge now, no succour from above,
Great Jove deserts me, and the son of Jove,
Propitious once, and kind ! Then welcome fate !   385

'Tis true I perish, yet I perish great:
Yet in a mighty deed I shall expire,
Let future ages hear it, and admire !'
    Fierce, at the word, his weighty sword he drew,
And, all collected, on Achilles flew. 390
So Jove's bold bird, high balanced in the air,
Stoops from the clouds to truss the quivering hare.
Nor less Achilles his fierce soul prepares ;
Before his breast the flaming shield he bears,
Refulgent orb ! above his fourfold cone 395
The gilded horse-hair sparkled in the sun,
Nodding at every step, (Vulcanian frame !)
And as he mov'd, his figure seem'd on flame.
As radiant Hesper shines with keener light,
Far-beaming o'er the silver host of night, 400
When all the starry train emblaze the sphere :
So shone the point of great Achilles' spear.
In his right hand he waves the weapon round,
Eyes the whole man, and meditates the wound :
But the rich mail Patroclus lately wore, 405
Securely cased the warrior's body o'er.
One place at length he spies, to let in fate,
Where 'twixt the neck and throat the jointed plate
Gave entrance : through that penetrable part
Furious he drove the well-directed dart : 410
Nor pierced the windpipe yet, nor took the power
Of speech, unhappy ! from thy dying hour.
Prone on the field the bleeding warrior lies,
While thus, triumphing, stern Achilles cries :
    " At last is Hector stretch'd upon the plain, 415
Who fear'd no vengeance for Patroclus slain :

Then prince ! you should have fear'd, what now you feel ;
Achilles absent was Achilles still.
Yet a short space the great avenger stay'd,
Then low in dust thy strength and glory laid.   420
Peaceful he sleeps, with all our rites adorn'd,
For ever honour'd, and for ever mourn'd :
While, cast to all the rage of hostile power,
Thee birds shall mangle, and the dogs devour."
    Then Hector, fainting at th' approach of death :   425
" By thy own soul ! by those who gave thee breath !
By all the sacred prevalence of prayer ;
Ah, leave me not for Grecian dogs to tear !
The common rites of sepulture bestow,
To soothe a father's and a mother's woe ;   430
Let their large gifts procure an urn at least,
And Hector's ashes in his country rest."
    " No, wretch accurs'd ! " relentless he replies,
(Flames, as he spoke, shot flashing from his eyes,)
Not those who gave me breath should bid me spare,   435
Nor all the sacred prevalence of prayer.
Could I myself the bloody banquet join !
No — to the dogs that carcass I resign.
Should Troy to bribe me bring forth all her store,
And, giving thousands, offer thousands more ;   440
Should Dardan Priam, and his weeping dame,
Drain their whole realm to buy one funeral flame ;
Their Hector on the pile they should not see,
Nor rob the vultures of one limb of thee."
    Then thus the chief his dying accents drew :   445
" Thy rage, implacable ! too well I knew :
The Furies that relentless breast have steel'd

And curs'd thee with a heart that cannot yield.
Yet think, a day will come, when Fate's decree
And angry gods shall wreak this wrong on thee;   450
Phœbus and Paris shall avenge my fate,
And stretch thee here, before this Scæan gate."
    He ceas'd: the fates suppress'd his labouring breath,
And his eyes stiffen'd at the hand of death;
To the dark realm the spirit wings its way,   455
(The manly body left a load of clay,)
And plaintive glides along the dreary coast,
A naked, wandering, melancholy ghost!
    Achilles, musing as he roll'd his eyes
O'er the dead hero, thus (unheard) replies: 460
"Die thou the first! when Jove and heaven ordain,
I follow thee."   He said, and stripp'd the slain.
Then, forcing backward from the gaping wound
The reeking javelin, cast it on the ground.
The thronging Greeks behold with wondering eyes   465
His manly beauty, and superior size:
While some, ignobler, the great dead deface
With wounds ungenerous, or with taunts disgrace.
"How changed that Hector! who, like Jove, of late
Sent lightning on our fleets and scatter'd fate!"   470
    High o'er the slain the great Achilles stands,
Begirt with heroes and surrounding bands;
And thus aloud, while all the host attends:
"Princes and leaders! countrymen and friends!
Since now at length the powerful will of heaven   475
The dire destroyer to our arm has given,
Is not Troy fall'n already?   Haste, ye powers!
See if already their deserted towers

F

Are left unmann'd ; or if they yet retain
The souls of heroes, their great Hector slain?   480
But what is Troy, or glory what to me?
Or why reflects my mind on aught but thee,
Divine Patroclus ! death has seal'd his eyes ;
Unwept, unhonour'd, uninterr'd he lies !
Can his dear image from my soul depart,   485
Long as the vital spirit moves my heart?
If, in the melancholy shades below,
The flames of friends and lovers cease to glow,
Yet mine shall sacred last; mine, undecay'd,
Burn on through death, and animate my shade.   490
Meanwhile, ye sons of Greece, in triumph bring
The corse of Hector, and your Pæans sing.
Be this the song, slow moving tow'rd the shore,
' Hector is dead, and Ilion is no more.' "

    Then his fell soul a thought of vengeance bred ;   495
(Unworthy of himself, and of the dead ;)
The nervous ancles bor'd, his feet he bound
With thongs inserted through the double wound ;
These fix'd up high behind the rolling wain,
His graceful head was trailed along the plain.   500
Proud on his car th' insulting victor stood,
And bore aloft his arms, distilling blood.
He smites the steeds ; the rapid chariot flies ;
The sudden clouds of circling dust arise.
Now lost is all that formidable air ;   505
The face divine, and long-descending hair,
Purple the ground, and streak the sable sand ;
Deform'd, dishonour'd, in his native land !
Given to the rage of an insulting throng !

Friedrich Preller.

ILIAD — BOOK XXII., 495–510.

And, in his parents' sight, now dragg'd along.   510
  The mother first beheld with sad survey ;
She rent her tresses, venerably grey,
And cast far off the regal veils away.
With piercing shrieks his bitter fate she moans,
While the sad father answers groans with groans ,   515
Tears after tears his mournful cheeks o'erflow,
And the whole city wears one face of woe :
No less than if the rage of hostile fires,
From her foundations curling to her spires
O'er the proud citadel at length should rise,   520
And the last blaze send Ilion to the skies.
The wretched monarch of the falling state,
Distracted, presses to the Dardan gate :
Scarce the whole people stop his desperate course,
While strong affliction gives the feeble force :   525
Grief tears his heart, and drives him to and fro,
In all the raging impotence of woe.
At length he roll'd in dust, and thus begun,
Imploring all, and naming one by one :
" Ah ! let me, let me go where sorrow calls ;   530
I, only I, will issue from your walls,
(Guide or companion, friends ! I ask ye none,)
And bow before the murderer of my son.
My grief perhaps his pity may engage ;
Perhaps at least he may respect my age.   535
He has a father, too ; a man like me ;
One, not exempt from age and misery :
(Vig'rous no more, as when his young embrace
Begot this pest of me, and all my race.)
How many valiant sons, in early bloom,   540

Has that curs'd hand sent headlong to the tomb!
Thee, Hector! last; thy loss (divinely brave!)
Sinks my sad soul with sorrow to the grave.
Oh had thy gentle spirit pass'd in peace,
The son expiring in the sire's embrace,   545
While both thy parents wept thy fatal hour,
And, bending o'er thee, mix'd the tender shower!
Some comfort that had been, some sad relief,
To melt in full satiety of grief!"

   Thus wail'd the father, grovelling on the ground,   550
And all the eyes of Ilion stream'd around.

   Amidst her matrons Hecuba appears:
(A mourning princess, and a train in tears:)
"Ah! why has heaven prolong'd this hated breath,
Patient of horrors, to behold thy death?   555
O Hector! late thy parents' pride and joy,
The boast of nations! the defence of Troy!
To whom her safety and her fame she owed,
Her chief, her hero, and almost her god!
O fatal change! become in one sad day   560
A senseless corse! inanimated clay!"

   But not as yet the fatal news had spread
To fair Andromache, of Hector dead;
As yet no messenger had told his fate,
Nor e'en his stay without the Scæan gate.   565
Far in the close recesses of the dome
Pensive she plied the melancholy loom;
A growing work employ'd her secret hours,
Confus'dly gay with intermingled flowers.
Her fair-hair'd handmaids heat the brazen urn,   570
The bath preparing for her lord's return:

In vain : alas ! her lord returns no more !
Unbathed he lies, and bleeds along the shore !
Now from the walls the clamours reach her ear
And all her members shake with sudden fear ;   575
Forth from her ivory hand the shuttle falls,
As thus, astonish'd, to her maids she calls :
　"Ah, follow me !" (she cried ;) "what plaintive noise
Invades my ear?   'Tis sure my mother's voice.
My faltering knees their trembling frame desert,   580
A pulse unusual flutters at my heart.
Some strange disaster, some reverse of fate
(Ye gods avert it !) threats the Trojan state.
Far be the omen which my thoughts suggest !
But much I fear my Hector's dauntless breast   585
Confronts Achilles ; chas'd along the plain,
Shut from our walls ! I fear, I fear him slain !
Safe in the crowd he ever scorn'd to wait,
And sought for glory in the jaws of fate :
Perhaps that noble heat has cost his breath,   590
Now quench'd for ever in the arms of death."
　She spoke ; and, furious, with distracted pace,
Fears in her heart, and anguish in her face,
Flies through the dome, (the maids her steps pursue,)
And mounts the walls, and sends around her view.   595
Too soon her eyes the killing object found,
The godlike Hector dragged along the ground.
· A sudden darkness shades her swimming eyes :
She faints, she falls ; her breath, her colour, flies.
Her hair's fair ornaments, the braids that bound,   600
The net that held them, and the wreath that crown'd,
The veil and diadem, flew far away ;

(The gift of Venus on her bridal day.)
Around, a train of weeping sisters stands,
To raise her sinking with assistant hands.   605
Scarce from the verge of death recall'd, again
She faints, or but recovers to complain :
   "O wretched husband of a wretched wife !
Born with one fate, to one unhappy life !
For sure one star its baneful beam display'd   610
On Priam's roof, and Hippoplacia's shade.
From different parents, different climes, we came,
At different periods, yet our fate the same !
Why was my birth to great Eëtion ow'd,
And why was all that tender care bestow'd?   615
Would I had never been ! — Oh thou, the ghost
Of my dead husband ! miserably lost !
Thou to the dismal realms for ever gone !
And I abandon'd, desolate, alone !
An only child, once comfort of my pains,   620
Sad product now of hapless love, remains !
No more to smile upon his sire ! no friend
To help him now ! no father to defend !
For should he 'scape the sword, the common doom,
What wrongs attend him, and what griefs to come !   625
E'en from his own paternal roof expell'd,
Some stranger ploughs his patrimonial field.
The day that to the shades the father sends,
Robs the sad orphan of his father's friends :
He, wretched outcast of mankind ! appears   630
For ever sad, for ever bathed in tears;
Amongst the happy, unregarded he
Hangs on the robe or trembles at the knee;

While those his father's former bounty fed,
Nor reach the goblet, nor divide the bread: 635
The kindest but his present wants allay,
To leave him wretched the succeeding day.
Frugal compassion!   Heedless, they who boast
Both parents still, nor feel what he has lost,
Shall cry, 'Begone! thy father feasts not here:'   640
The wretch obeys, retiring with a tear.
Thus wretched, thus retiring all in tears,
To my sad soul Astyanax appears!
Forced by repeated insults to return,
And to his widow'd mother vainly mourn.   645
He who, with tender delicacy bred,
With princes sported, and on dainties fed,
And, when still evening gave him up to rest
Sunk soft in down upon the nurse's breast,
Must — ah what must he not?   Whom Ilion calls   650
Astyanax, from her well-guarded walls,
Is now that name no more, unhappy boy!
Since now no more thy father guards his Troy.
But thou, my Hector! liest expos'd in air,
Far from thy parents' and thy consort's care,   655
Whose hand in vain, directed by her love,
The martial scarf and robe of triumph wove.
Now to devouring flames be these a prey,
Useless to thee, from this accursed day!
Yet let the sacrifice at least be paid,   660
An honour to the living, not the dead!"
    So spake the mournful dame: her matrons hear,
Sigh back her sighs, and answer tear with tear.

J. Flaxman and A. Schill.

BOOK XXIV.

THE REDEMPTION OF THE BODY OF HECTOR.

Now from the finish'd games the Grecian band
Seek their black ships, and clear the crowded strand :
All stretch'd at ease the genial banquet share,
And pleasing slumbers quiet all their care.
Not so Achilles : he, to grief resign'd,   5
His friend's dear image present to his mind,
Takes his sad couch, more unobserv'd to weep,
Nor tastes the gifts of all-composing sleep ;
Restless he roll'd around his weary bed,
And all his soul on his Patroclus fed :   10
The form so pleasing, and the heart so kind,
That youthful vigour, and that manly mind,
What toils they shar'd, what martial works they wrought,
What seas they measur'd, and what fields they fought ;

All pass'd before him in remembrance dear,   15
Thought follows thought, and tear succeeds to tear.
And now supine, now prone, the hero lay,
Now shifts his side, impatient for the day;
Then starting up, disconsolate he goes
Wide on the lonely beach to vent his woes.   20
There as the solitary mourner raves,
The ruddy morning rises o'er the waves :
. Soon as it rose, his furious steeds he join'd ;
The chariot flies, and Hector trails behind.
And thrice, Patroclus ! round thy monument   25
Was Hector dragg'd, then hurried to the tent.
There sleep at last o'ercomes the hero's eyes ;
While foul in dust th' unhonour'd carcass lies,
But not deserted by the pitying skies.
For Phœbus watch'd it with superior care,   30
Preserv'd from gaping wounds, and tainting air ;
And, ignominious as it swept the field,
Spread o'er the sacred corse his golden shield.
All heaven was mov'd, and Hermes will'd to go
By stealth to snatch him from th' insulting foe ;   35
But Neptune this, and Pallas this denies,
And th' unrelenting empress of the skies :
E'er since that day implacable to Troy,
What time young Paris, simple shepherd boy,
Won by destructive lust (reward obscene)   40
Their charms rejected for the Cyprian queen.
But when the tenth celestial morning broke,
To heaven assembled, thus Apollo spoke :
    " Unpitying powers ! how oft each holy fane
Has Hector tinged with blood of victims slain ?   45

And can ye still his cold remains pursue?
Still grudge his body to the Trojans' view?
Deny to consort, mother, son, and sire,
The last sad honours of a funeral fire?
Is then the dire Achilles all your care?   50
That iron heart, inflexibly severe ;
A lion, not a man, who slaughters wide
In strength of rage and impotence of pride ;
Who hastes to murder with a savage joy,
Invades around, and breathes but to destroy.   55
Shame is not of his soul, nor understood,
The greatest evil and the greatest good.
Still for one loss he rages unresign'd,
Repugnant to the lot of all mankind ;
To lose a friend, a brother, or a son,   60
Heaven dooms each mortal, and its will is done :
Awhile they sorrow, then dismiss their care ;
Fate gives the wound, and man is born to bear.
But this insatiate the commission given
By fate exceeds, and tempts the wrath of heaven :   65
Lo how his rage dishonest drags along
Hector's dead earth, insensible of wrong !
Brave though he be, yet by no reason aw'd,
He violates the laws of man and God !"
    " If equal honours by the partial skies   70
Are doom'd both heroes," (Juno thus replies,)
" If Thetis' son must no distinction know,
Then hear, ye gods ! the patron of the bow.
But Hector only boasts a mortal claim,
His birth deriving from a mortal dame :   75
Achilles of your own ethereal race

Springs from a goddess, by a man's embrace :
(A goddess by ourself to Peleus given,
A man divine, and chosen friend of heaven :)
To grace those nuptials, from the bright abode 80
Yourselves were present ; where this minstrel-god
(Well-pleas'd to share the feast) amid the quire
Stood proud to hymn, and tune his youthful lyre."
    Then thus the Thunderer checks the imperial dame :
" Let not thy wrath the court of heaven inflame ; 85
Their merits, nor their honours, are the same.
But mine, and every god's peculiar grace
Hector deserves, of all the Trojan race :
Still on our shrines his grateful offerings lay
(The only honours men to gods can pay,) 90
Nor ever from our smoking altar ceas'd
The pure libation, and the holy feast.
Howe'er, by stealth to snatch the corse away,
We will not : Thetis guards it night and day.
But haste, and summon to our courts above 95
The azure queen : let her persuasion move
Her furious son from Priam to receive
The proffer'd ransom, and the corse to leave."
    He added not : and Iris from the skies,
Swift as a whirlwind, on the message flies ; 100
Meteorous the face of ocean sweeps,
Refulgent gliding o'er the sable deeps.
Between where Samos wide his forests spreads,
And rocky Imbrus lifts its pointed heads,
Down plunged the maid ; (the parted waves resound ;) 105
She plunged, and instant shot the dark profound.
As, bearing death in the fallacious bait,

From the bent angle sinks the leaden weight;
So pass'd the goddess through the closing wave,
Where Thetis sorrow'd in her secret cave :   110
There placed amidst her melancholy train
(The blue-hair'd sisters of the sacred main)
Pensive she sat, revolving fates to come,
And wept her godlike son's approaching doom.
    Then thus the goddess of the painted bow :   115
" Arise, O Thetis ! from thy seats below ;
'Tis Jove that calls."   " And why," (the dame replies)
" Calls Jove his Thetis to the hated skies?
Sad object as I am for heavenly sight !
Ah ! may my sorrows ever shun the light !   120
Howe'er, be heaven's almighty sire obeyed."
She spake, and veil'd her head in sable shade,
Which, flowing long, her graceful person clad ;
And forth she paced majestically sad.
    Then through the world of waters they repair   125
(The way fair Iris led) to upper air.
The deeps dividing, o'er the coast they rise,
And touch with momentary flight the skies.
There in the lightning's blaze the sire they found,
And all the gods in shining synod round.   130
Thetis approach'd with anguish in her face,
(Minerva rising gave the mourner place,)
E'en Juno sought her sorrows to console,
And offer'd from her hand the nectar bowl :
She tasted, and resign'd it : then began   135
The sacred sire of gods and mortal man :
" Thou com'st, fair Thetis, but with grief o'ercast,
Maternal sorrows, long, ah long to last !

Suffice, we know, and we partake, thy cares :
But yield to fate, and hear what Jove declares.   140
Nine days are past, since all the court above
In Hector's cause have mov'd the ear of Jove ;
'Twas voted, Hermes from his godlike foe
By stealth should bear him, but we will'd not so :
We will, thy son himself the corse restore,   145
And to his conquest add this glory more.
Then hie thee to him, and our mandate bear ;
Tell him he tempts the wrath of heaven too far :
Nor let him more (our anger if he dread)
Vent his mad vengeance on the sacred dead :   150
But yield to ransom and the father's prayer.
The mournful father Iris shall prepare,
With gifts to sue ; and offer to his hands
Whate'er his honour asks or heart demands."

His word the silver-footed queen attends,   155
And from Olympus' snowy tops descends.
Arriv'd, she heard the voice of loud lament,
And echoing groans that shook the lofty tent.
His friends prepare the victim and dispose
Repast unheeded, while he vents his woes.   160
The goddess seats her by her pensive son ;
She press'd his hand, and tender thus begun :
" How long, unhappy ! shall thy sorrows flow?
And thy heart waste with life-consuming woe?
Mindless of food, or love, whose pleasing reign   165
Soothes weary life, and softens human pain.
O snatch the moments yet within thy power ;
Not long to live, indulge the amorous hour !
Lo ! Jove himself (for Jove's command I bear,)

Forbids to tempt the wrath of heaven too far.   170
No longer then, (his fury if thou dread)
Detain the relics of great Hector dead ;
Nor vent on senseless earth thy vengeance vain,
But yield to ransom and restore the slain."
    To whom Achilles : " Be the ransom given,   175
And we submit, since such the will of heaven."
    While thus they commun'd, from th' Olympian bowers
Jove orders Iris to the Trojan towers :
" Haste, wingèd goddess, to the sacred town,
And urge her monarch to redeem his son ;   180
Alone, the Ilian ramparts let him leave,
And bear what stern Achilles may receive :
Alone, for so we will : no Trojan near ;
Except, to place the dead with decent care,
Some aged herald, who, with gentle hand,   185
May the slow mules and funeral car command.
Nor let him death, nor let him danger dread,
Safe through the foe by our protection led :
Him Hermes to Achilles shall convey,
Guard of his life, and partner of his way.   190
Fierce as he is, Achilles' self shall spare
His age, nor touch one venerable hair :
Some thought there must be in a soul so brave,
Some sense of duty, some desire to save."
    Then down her bow the wingèd Iris drives,   195
And swift at Priam's mournful court arrives :
Where the sad sons beside their father's throne
Sat bathed in tears, and answered groan with groan.
And all amidst them lay the hoary sire,
(Sad scene of woe !) his face, his wrapp'd attire   200

Conceal'd from sight ; with frantic hands he spread
A shower of ashes o'er his neck and head.
From room to room his pensive daughters roam :
Whose shrieks and clamours fill the vaulted dome ;
Mindful of those, who, late their pride and joy,   205
Lie pale and breathless round the fields of Troy !
Before the king Jove's messenger appears,
And thus in whispers greets his trembling ears :
    " Fear not, oh father ! no ill news I bear ;
From Jove I come, Jove makes thee still his care ;   210
For Hector's sake these walls he bids thee leave,
And bear what stern Achilles may receive :
Alone, for so he wills : no Trojan near,
Except, to place the dead with decent care,
Some aged herald, who, with gentle hand,   215
May the slow mules and funeral car command.
Nor shalt thou death, nor shalt thou danger dread ;
Safe through the foe by his protection led :
Thee Hermes to Pelides shall convey,
Guard of thy life, and partner of thy way.   220
Fierce as he is, Achilles' self shall spare
Thy age, nor touch one venerable hair :
Some thought there must be in a soul so brave,
Some sense of duty, some desire to save."
    She spoke, and vanish'd.   Priam bids prepare   225
His gentle mules, and harness to the car ;
There, for the gifts, a polish'd casket lay ;
His pious sons the king's commands obey.
Then pass'd the monarch to his bridal-room,
Where cedar-beams the lofty roofs perfume,   230
And where the treasures of his empire lay ;

Then call'd his queen, and thus began to say:
  "Unhappy consort of a king distress'd!
Partake the troubles of thy husband's breast:
I saw descend the messenger of Jove,   235
Who bids me try Achilles' mind to move,
Forsake these ramparts, and with gifts obtain
The corse of Hector, at yon navy slain.
Tell me thy thought: my heart impels to go
Through hostile camps, and bears me to the foe."   240
  The hoary monarch thus: her piercing cries
Sad Hecuba renews, and then replies:
" Ah! whither wanders thy distemper'd mind;
And where the prudence now that awed mankind,
Through Phrygia once, and foreign regions known?   245
Now all confus'd, distracted, overthrown!
Singly to pass through hosts of foes! to face
(Oh heart of steel!) the murderer of thy race!
To view that deathful eye, and wander o'er
Those hands, yet red with Hector's noble gore!   250
Alas! my lord! he knows not how to spare,
And what his mercy thy slain sons declare;
So brave! so many fall'n! to calm his rage
Vain were thy dignity, and vain thy age.
No — pent in this sad palace, let us give   255
To grief the wretched days we have to live.
Still, still, for Hector let our sorrows flow,
Born to his own, and to his parents' woe!
Doom'd from the hour his luckless life begun,
To dogs, to vultures, and to Peleus' son!   260
Oh! in his dearest blood might I allay
My rage, and these barbarities repay!

For ah ! could Hector merit thus? whose breath
Expir'd not meanly, in inactive death :
He pour'd his latest blood in manly fight,   265
And fell a hero in his country's right."
   "Seek not to stay me, nor my soul affright
With words of omen, like a bird of night,"
(Replied unmov'd the venerable man :)
   " 'Tis heaven commands me, and you urge in vain.   270
Had any mortal voice th' injunction laid,
Nor augur, priest, nor seer had been obey'd.
A present goddess brought the high command :
I saw, I heard her, and the word shall stand.
I go, ye gods ! obedient to your call :   275
If in yon camp your powers have doom'd my fall,
Content : by the same hand let me expire !
Add to the slaughter'd son the wretched sire !
One cold embrace at least may be allow'd,
And my last tears flow mingled with his blood ! "   280
   Forth from his open'd stores, this said, he drew
Twelve costly carpets of refulgent hue ;
As many vests, as many mantles told,
And twelve fair veils, and garments stiff with gold ;
Two tripods next, and twice two chargers shine,   285
With ten pure talents from the richest mine ;
And last a large, well-labour'd bowl had place,
(The pledge of treaties once with friendly Thrace ;)
Seem'd all too mean the stores he could employ,
For one last look to buy him back to Troy !   290
   Lo ! the sad father, frantic with his pain,
Around him furious drives his menial train :
In vain each slave with duteous care attends,
   G

Each office hurts him, and each face offends.
"What make ye here, officious crowds!" (he cries)   295
"Hence, nor obtrude your anguish on my eyes.
Have ye no griefs at home, to fix ye there?
Am I the only object of despair?
Am I become my people's common show,
Set up by Jove your spectacle of woe?   300
No, you must feel him too: yourselves must fall:
The same stern god to ruin gives you all:
Nor is great Hector lost by me alone:
Your sole defence, your guardian power, is gone!
I see your blood the fields of Phrygia drown;   305
I see the ruins of your smoking town!
Oh send me, gods, ere that sad day shall come,
A willing ghost to Pluto's dreary dome!"
    He said, and feebly drives his friends away:
The sorrowing friends his frantic rage obey.   310
Next on his sons his erring fury falls,
Polites, Paris, Agathon, he calls;
His threats Deïphobus and Dius hear,
Hippothoüs, Pammon, Helenus the seer,
And generous Antiphon; for yet these nine   315
Surviv'd, sad relics of his numerous line:
    "Inglorious sons of an unhappy sire!
Why did not all in Hector's cause expire?
Wretch that I am! my bravest offspring slain,
You, the disgrace of Priam's house, remain!   320
Nestor the brave, renown'd in ranks of war,
With Troilus, dreadful on his rushing car,
And last great Hector, more than man divine,
For sure he seem'd not of terrestrial line!

Friedrich Preller.

ILIAD — BOOK XXIV., 331–406.

All those relentless Mars untimely slew,   325
And left me these, a soft and servile crew,
Whose days the feast and wanton dance employ,
Gluttons and flatterers, the contempt of Troy!
Why teach ye not my rapid wheels to run,
And speed my journey to redeem my son?"   330
   The sons their father's wretched age revere,
Forgive his anger, and produce the car.
High on the seat the cabinet they bind:
The new-made car with solid beauty shined:
Box was the yoke, embossed with costly pains,   335
And hung with ringlets to receive the reins:
Nine cubits long, the traces swept the ground;
These to the chariot's polish'd pole they bound,
Then fix'd a ring the running reins to guide,
And, close beneath, the gather'd ends were tied.   340
Next with the gifts (the price of Hector slain)
The sad attendants load the groaning wain:
Last to the yoke the well-match'd mules they bring,
(The gift of Mysia to the Trojan king.)
But the fair horses, long his darling care,   345
Himself receiv'd, and harness'd to his car:
Griev'd as he was, he not this task denied;
The hoary herald helped him at his side.
While careful these the gentle coursers join'd,
Sad Hecuba approach'd with anxious mind;   350
A golden bowl, that foam'd with fragrant wine,
(Libation destin'd to the power divine,)
Held in her right, before the steeds she stands,
And thus consigns it to the monarch's hands:
   "Take this, and pour to Jove; that, safe from harms, 355

His grace restore thee to our roof and arms.
Since, victor of thy fears, and slighting mine,
Heaven, or thy soul, inspire this bold design,
Pray to that god, who, high on Ida's brow
Surveys thy desolated realms below,   360
His wingèd messenger to send from high,
And lead the way with heavenly augury:
Let the strong sovereign of the plumy race
Tower on the right of yon ethereal space.
That sign beheld, and strengthen'd from above,   365
Boldly pursue the journey mark'd by Jove;.
But if the god his augury denies,
Suppress thy impulse, nor reject advice."
   " 'Tis just" (said Priam) " to the Sire above
To raise our hands; for who so good as Jove?"   370
   He spoke, and bade th' attendant handmaid bring
The purest water of the living spring;
(Her ready hands the ewer and bason held;)
Then took the golden cup his queen had fill'd;
On the mid pavement pours the rosy wine,   375
Uplifts his eyes, and calls the power divine:
   " Oh first and greatest! heaven's imperial lord!
On lofty Ida's holy hill adored!
To stern Achilles now direct my ways,
And teach him mercy when a father prays.   380
If such thy will, despatch from yonder sky
Thy sacred bird, celestial augury!
Let the strong sovereign of the plumy race
Tower on the right of yon ethereal space:
So shall thy suppliant, strengthen'd from above,   385
Fearless pursue the journey mark'd by Jove."

Jove heard his prayer, and from the throne on high
Despatch'd his bird, celestial augury!
The swift-wing'd chaser of the feather'd game,
And known to gods by Percnos' lofty name. 390
Wide as appears some palace-gate display'd,
So broad his pinions stretch'd their ample shade,
As, stooping dexter with resounding wings,
Th' imperial bird descends in airy rings.
A dawn of joy in every face appears; 395
The mourning matron dries her timorous tears.
Swift on his car th' impatient monarch sprung;
The brazen portal in his passage rung.
The mules preceding draw the loaded wain,
Charged with the gifts; Idæus holds the rein: 400
The king himself his gentle steeds controls,
And through surrounding friends the chariot rolls;
On his slow wheels the following people wait,
Mourn at each step, and give him up to fate;
With hands uplifted, eye him as he pass'd, 405
And gaze upon him as they gaz'd their last.
   Now forward fares the father on his way,
Through the lone fields, and back to Ilion they.
Great Jove beheld him as he cross'd the plain,
And felt the woes of miserable man. 410
Then thus to Hermes: "Thou, whose constant cares
Still succour mortals, and attend their prayers!
Behold an object to thy charge consign'd;
If ever pity touch'd thee for mankind,
Go, guard the sire; th' observing foe prevent, 415
And safe conduct him to Achilles' tent."
   The god obeys, his golden pinions binds,

And mounts incumbent on the wings of winds,
That high through fields of air his flight sustain,
O'er the wide earth, and o'er the boundless main: 420
Then grasps the wand that causes sleep to fly,
Or in soft slumbers seals the wakeful eye :
Thus arm'd, swift Hermes steers his airy way,
And stoops on Hellespont's resounding sea.
A beauteous youth, majestic and divine,   425
He seem'd ; fair offspring of some princely line !
Now twilight veil'd the glaring face of day,
And clad the dusky fields in sober grey ;
What time the herald and the hoary king,
Their chariot stopping at the silver spring,   430
That circling Ilus' ancient marble flows,
Allow'd their mules and steeds a short repose.
Through the dim shade the herald first espies
A man's approach, and thus to Priam cries :
" I mark some foe's advance : O king ! beware ;   435
This hard adventure claims thy utmost care ;
For much I fear destruction hovers nigh :
Our state asks counsel.   Is it best to fly?
Or, old and helpless, at his feet to fall,
(Two wretched suppliants) and for mercy call?"   440
    Th' afflicted monarch shiver'd with despair ;
Pale grew his face, and upright stood his hair ;
Sunk was his heart ; his colour went and came ;
A sudden trembling shook his aged frame :
When Hermes, greeting, touch'd his royal hand,   445
And, gentle, thus accosts with kind demand :
    " Say whither, father ! when each mortal sight
Is seal'd in sleep, thou wander'st through the night?

Why roam thy mules and steeds the plains along,
Through Grecian foes, so numerous and so strong?   450
What couldst thou hope, should these thy treasures view :
These, who with endless hate thy race pursue?
For what defence, alas ! couldst thou provide?
Thyself not young, a weak old man thy guide.
Yet suffer not thy soul to sink with dread ;   455
From me no harm shall touch thy reverend head :
From Greece I'll guard thee too ; for in those lines
The living image of my father shines."

　　" Thy words, that speak benevolence of mind,
Are true, my son ! " (the godlike sire rejoin'd :)   460
" Great are my hazards ; but the gods survey
My steps and send thee, guardian of my way.
Hail ! and be blest ; for scarce of mortal kind
Appear thy form, thy feature, and thy mind."

　　" Nor true are all thy words, nor erring wide,"   465
(The sacred messenger of heaven replied :)
" But say, convey'st thou through the lonely plains
What yet most precious of thy store remains,
To lodge in safety with some friendly hand?
Prepar'd perchance to leave thy native land?   470
Or fly'st thou now?　What hopes can Troy retain,
Thy matchless son, her guard and glory, slain?"

　　The king, alarmed : " Say what and whence thou art,
Who search the sorrows of a parent's heart,
And know so well how godlike Hector died?"   475
Thus Priam spoke, and Hermes thus replied :

　　" You tempt me, father, and with pity touch :
On this sad subject you inquire too much.
Oft have these eyes the godlike Hector view'd

In glorious fight, with Grecian blood imbrued ;   480
I saw him when, like Jove, his flames he toss'd
On thousand ships, and wither'd half a host :
I saw, but help'd not, stern Achilles' ire
Forbade assistance, and enjoy'd the fire.
For him I serve, of Myrmidonian race ;   485
One ship convey'd us from our native place ;
Polyctor is my sire, an honoured name,
Old like thyself, and not unknown to fame ;
Of seven his sons, by whom the lot was cast
To serve our prince, it fell on me the last.   490
To watch this quarter my adventure falls ;
For with the morn, the Greeks attack your walls ;
Sleepless they sit, impatient to engage,
And scarce their rulers check their martial rage."
    "If then thou art of stern Pelides' train,"   495
(The mournful monarch thus rejoin'd again,)
"Ah, tell me truly, where, oh ! where are laid
My son's dear relics? what befalls him dead?
Have dogs dismember'd on the naked plains,
Or yet unmangled rest his cold remains?"   500
    "O favour'd of the skies !" (thus answer'd then
The power that mediates between gods and men,)
"Nor dogs, nor vultures, have thy Hector rent,
But whole he lies, neglected in the tent :
This the twelfth evening since he rested there,   505
Untouch'd by worms, untainted by the air.
Still as Aurora's ruddy beam is spread,
Round his friend's tomb Achilles drags the dead ;
Yet undisfigur'd, or in limb or face,
All fresh he lies, with every living grace,   510

Majestical in death !   No stains are found
O'er all the corse, and closed is every wound ;
Though many a wound they gave.   Some heavenly care,
Some hand divine, preserves him ever fair :
Or all the host of heaven, to whom he led   515
A life so grateful, still regard him dead."
    Thus spoke to Priam the celestial guide,
And joyful thus the royal sire replied :
" Bless'd is the man who pays the gods above
The constant tribute of respect and love !   520
Those who inhabit the Olympian bower
My son forgot not, in exalted power ;
And Heaven, that every virtue bears in mind,
E'en to the ashes of the dust is kind.
But thou, oh generous youth ! this goblet take,   525
A pledge of gratitude for Hector's sake ;
And while the favouring gods our steps survey,
Safe to Pelides' tent conduct my way."
    To whom the latent god : " O king, forbear
To tempt my youth, for apt is youth to err ;   530
But can I, absent from my prince's sight,
Take gifts in secret, that must shun the light ?
What from our master's interest thus we draw,
Is but a licens'd theft that 'scapes the law.
Respecting him, my soul abjures th' offence ;   535
And, as the crime, I dread the consequence.
Thee, far as Argos, pleas'd I could convey ;
Guard of thy life, and partner of thy way :
On thee attend, thy safety to maintain,
O'er pathless forests, or the roaring main."   540
    He said, then took the chariot at a bound,

And snatch'd the reins, and whirl'd the lash around :
Before th' inspiring god that urged them on
The coursers fly, with spirit not their own.
And now they reach'd the naval walls, and found   545
The guards repasting, while the bowls go round :
On these the virtue of his wand he tries,
And pours deep slumber on their watchful eyes :
Then heav'd the massy gates, remov'd the bars,
And o'er the trenches led the rolling cars.   550
Unseen, through all the hostile camp they went,
And now approach'd Pelides' lofty tent.
Of fir the roof was raised, and cover'd o'er
With reeds collected from the marshy shore ;
And, fenced with palisades, a hall of state,   555
(The work of soldiers,) where the hero sat.
Large was the door, whose well-compacted strength
A solid pine tree barr'd of wondrous length ;
Scarce three strong Greeks could lift its mighty weight,
But great Achilles singly closed the gate.   560
This Hermes (such the power of gods) set wide ;
Then swift alighted the celestial guide,
And thus, reveal'd : " Hear, prince ! and understand
Thou ow'st thy guidance to no mortal hand ;
Hermes I am, descended from above,   565
The king of arts, the messenger of Jove.
Farewell : to shun Achilles' sight I fly ;
Uncommon are such favours of the sky,
Nor stand confess'd to frail mortality.
Now fearless enter, and prefer thy prayers ;   570
Adjure him by his father's silver hairs,
His son, his mother ! urge him to bestow

Whatever pity that stern heart can know."
  Thus having said, he vanish'd from his eyes,
And in a moment shot into the skies :   575
The king, confirm'd from heaven, alighted there,
And left his aged herald on the car.
With solemn pace through various rooms he went,
And found Achilles in his inner tent :
There sat the hero ; Alcimus the brave,   580
And great Automedon, attendance gave ;
These served his person at the royal feast ;
Around, at awful distance, stood the rest.
  Unseen by these, the king his entry made ;
And, prostrate now before Achilles laid,   585
Sudden (a venerable sight !) appears ;
Embraced his knees, and bath'd his hands in tears ;
Those direful hands his kisses press'd, imbrued
E'en with the best, the dearest of his blood !
  As when a wretch (who, conscious of his crime,   590
Pursued for murder, flies his native clime)
Just gains some frontier, breathless, pale, amaz'd !
All gaze, all wonder : thus Achilles gaz'd :
Thus stood th' attendants stupid with surprise :
All mute, yet seem'd to question with their eyes :   595
Each look'd on other, none the silence broke,
Till thus at last the kingly suppliant spoke :
  " Ah think, thou favour'd of the powers divine !
Think of thy father's age, and pity mine !
In me, that father's reverend image trace,   600
Those silver hairs, that venerable face ;
His trembling limbs, his helpless person, see !
In all my equal, but in misery !

Yet now, perhaps, some turn of human fate
Expels him helpless from his peaceful state ;   605
Think, from some powerful foe thou see'st him fly,
And beg protection with a feeble cry.
Yet still one comfort in his soul may rise ;
He hears his son still lives to glad his eyes ;
And, hearing, still may hope a better day   610
May send him thee, to chase that foe away.
No comfort to my griefs, no hopes remain,
The best, the bravest of my sons are slain !
Yet what a race ! ere Greece to Ilion came,
The pledge of many a lov'd and loving dame !   615
Nineteen one mother bore — Dead, all are dead !
How oft, alas ! has wretched Priam bled !
Still one was left, their loss to recompense ;
His father's hope, his country's last defence.
Him too thy rage has slain ! beneath thy steel,   620
Unhappy, in his country's cause, he fell !
For him through hostile camps I bent my way,
For him thus prostrate at thy feet I lay ;
Large gifts, proportion'd to thy wrath, I bear :
Oh, hear the wretched, and the gods revere !   625
Think of thy father, and this face behold !
See him in me, as helpless and as old ;
Though not so wretched : there he yields to me,
The first of men in sovereign misery.
Thus forced to kneel, thus grovelling to embrace,   630
The scourge and ruin of my realm and race :
Suppliant my children's murderer to implore,
And kiss those hands yet reeking with their gore ! "
    These words soft pity in the chief inspire,

Touch'd with the dear remembrance of his sire.   635
Then with his hand (as prostrate still he lay)
The old man's cheek he gently turn'd away,
Now each by turns indulged the gush of woe ;
And now the mingled tides together flow :
This low on earth, that gently bending o'er,   640
A father one, and one a son deplore :
But great Achilles different passions rend,
And now his sire he mourns, and now his friend.
Th' infectious softness through the heroes ran ;
One universal solemn shower began ;   645
They bore as heroes, but they felt as man.

   Satiate at length with unavailing woes,
From the high throne divine Achilles rose ;
The reverend monarch by the hand he rais'd ;
On his white beard and form majestic gaz'd,   650
Not unrelenting : then serene began
With words to soothe the miserable man :

   " Alas ! what weight of anguish hast thou known,
Unhappy prince ! thus guardless and alone
To pass through foes, and thus undaunted face   655
The man whose fury has destroy'd thy race !
Heaven sure has arm'd thee with a heart of steel,
A strength proportion'd to the woes you feel.
Rise then : let reason mitigate our care :
To mourn, avails not : man is born to bear.   660
Such is, alas ! the gods' severe decree ;
They, only they, are blest, and only free.
Two urns by Jove's high throne have ever stood,
The source of evil one, and one of good ;
From thence the cup of mortal man he fills,   665

Blessings to these, to those distributes ills;
To most he mingles both : the wretch decreed
To taste the bad, unmix'd, is curs'd indeed :
Pursued by wrongs, by meagre famine driven,
He wanders, outcast both of earth and heaven.   670
The happiest taste not happiness sincere,
But find the cordial draught is dash'd with care.
Who more than Peleus shone in wealth and power?
What stars concurring bless'd his natal hour !
A realm, a goddess, to his wishes given,   675
Graced by the gods with all the gifts of heaven !
One evil, yet, o'ertakes his latest day ;
No race succeeding to imperial sway :
An only son ! and he (alas !) ordain'd
To fall untimely in a foreign land !   680
See him, in Troy, the pious care decline
Of his weak age, to live the curse of thine !
Thou too, old man, hast happier days beheld ;
In riches once, in children once excell'd ;
Extended Phrygia own'd thy ample reign,   685
And all fair Lesbos' blissful seats contain,
And all wide Hellespont's unmeasur'd main.
But since the god his hand has pleas'd to turn,
And fill thy measure from his bitter urn,
What sees the sun, but hapless heroes' falls?   690
War, and the blood of men, surround thy walls !
What must be, must be.   Bear thy lot, nor shed
These unavailing sorrows o'er the dead ;
Thou canst not call him from the Stygian shore,
But thou, alas ! may'st live to suffer more ! "   695
    To whom the king : " O favour'd of the skies !

Here let me grow to earth ! since Hector lies
On the bare beach, depriv'd of obsequies.
O give me Hector : to my eyes restore
His corse, and take the gifts : I ask no more !   700
Thou, as thou may'st, these boundless stores enjoy ;
Safe may'st thou sail, and turn thy wrath from Troy ;
So shall thy pity and forbearance give
A weak old man to see the light, and live ! "
    " Move me no more," (Achilles thus replies,   705
While kindling anger sparkled in his eyes,)
" Nor seek by tears my steady soul to bend ;
To yield thy Hector I myself intend :
For know, from Jove my goddess-mother came ;
(Old Ocean's daughter, silver-footed dame ;)   710
Nor com'st thou but by heaven ; nor com'st alone ;
Some god impels with courage not thy own :
No human hand the weighty gates unbarr'd,
Nor could the boldest of our youth have dar'd
To pass our out-works, or elude the guard.   715
Cease ; lest, neglectful of high Jove's command,
I shew thee, king ! thou tread'st on hostile land ;
Release my knees, thy suppliant arts give o'er,
And shake the purpose of my soul no more."
    The sire obey'd him, trembling and o'eraw'd.   720
Achilles, like a lion, rush'd abroad ;
Automedon and Alcimus attend,
Whom most he honour'd, since he lost his friend ;
These to unyoke the mules and horses went,
And led the hoary herald to the tent :   725
Next, heap'd on high, the numerous presents bear
(Great Hector's ransom) from the polish'd car.

Two splendid mantles, and a carpet spread,
They leave, to cover and enwrap the dead :
Then call the handmaids, with assistant toil   730
To wash the body, and anoint with oil,
Apart from Priam ; lest th' unhappy sire,
Provok'd to passion, once more rouse to ire
The stern Pelides ; and nor sacred age,
Nor Jove's command, should check the rising rage.   735
This done, the garments o'er the corse they spread;
Achilles lifts it to the funeral bed :
Then, while the body on the car they laid,
He groans, and calls on lov'd Patroclus' shade :

"If, in that gloom which never light must know,   740
The deeds of mortals touch the ghosts below ;
O friend ! forgive me that I thus fulfil
(Restoring Hector) heaven's unquestion'd will.
The gifts the father gave, be ever thine,
To grace thy manes, and adorn thy shrine."   745

He said, and, entering, took his seat of state,
Where full before him reverend Priam sate :
To whom, compos'd, the godlike chief begun :
"Lo ! to thy prayer restor'd, thy breathless son ;
Extended on the funeral couch he lies   750
And, soon as morning paints the eastern skies,
The sight is granted to thy longing eyes.
But now the peaceful hours of sacred night
Demand refection, and to rest invite :
Nor thou, O father ! thus consum'd with woe,   755
The common cares that nourish life forego.
Not thus did Niobe, of form divine,
A parent once, whose sorrows equall'd thine :

Six youthful sons, as many blooming maids,
In one sad day beheld the Stygian shades :   760
Those by Apollo's silver bow were slain,
These, Cynthia's arrows stretch'd upon the plain.
So was her pride chastis'd by wrath divine,
Who match'd her own with bright Latona's line ;
But two the goddess, twelve the queen enjoy'd ;   765
Those boasted twelve th' avenging two destroy'd.
Steep'd in their blood, and in the dust outspread,
Nine days, neglected, lay expos'd the dead ;
None by to weep them, to inhume them none ;
(For Jove had turn'd the nation all to stone ;)   770
The gods themselves, at length, relenting, gave
Th' unhappy race the honours of a grave.
Herself a rock (for such was heaven's high will)
Through deserts wild now pours a weeping rill ;
Where round the bed whence Acheloüs springs,   775
The watery fairies dance in mazy rings :
There, high on Sipylus's shaggy brow,
She stands, her own sad monument of woe ;
The rock for ever lasts, the tears for ever flow.
Such griefs, O king ! have other parents known :   780
Remember theirs, and mitigate thy own.
The care of heaven thy Hector has appear'd ;
Nor shall he lie unwept, and uninterr'd ;
Soon may thy aged cheeks in tears be drown'd,
And all the eyes of Ilion stream around."   785
   He said, and, rising, chose the victim ewe
With silver fleece, which his attendants slew.
The limbs they sever from the reeking hide,
With skill prepare them, and in parts divide :

H

Each on the coals the separate morsels lays,   790
And hasty snatches from the rising blaze.
With bread the glittering canisters they load,
Which round the board Automedon bestow'd :
The chief himself to each his portion placed,
And each indulging shar'd in sweet repast.   795
When now the rage of hunger was repress'd,
The wondering hero eyes his royal guest ;
No less the royal guest the hero eyes,
His godlike aspect, and majestic size ;
Here, youthful grace and noble fire engage,   800
And there, the mild benevolence of age.
Thus gazing long, the silence neither broke ;
(A solemn scene !) at length the father spoke :
    "Permit me now, belov'd of Jove, to steep
My careful temples in the dew of sleep :   805
For since the day that number'd with the dead
My hapless son, the dust has been my bed ;
Soft sleep a stranger to my weeping eyes ;
My only food, my sorrows and my sighs !
Till now, encourag'd by the grace you give,   810
I share thy banquet, and consent to live."
    With that, Achilles bade prepare the bed,
With purple soft, and shaggy carpets spread.
Forth, by the flaming lights, they bend their way,
And place the couches, and the coverings lay.   815
Then he : " Now, father, sleep, but sleep not here,
Consult thy safety, and forgive my fear
Lest any Argive, (at this hour awake,
To ask our counsel, or our orders take,)
Approaching sudden to our open'd tent,   820

Perchance behold thee, and our grace prevent.
Should such report thy honour'd person here,
The king of men the ransom might defer.
But say with speed, if aught of thy desire
Remains unask'd, what time the rites require   825
T' inter thy Hector?   For so long we stay
Our slaughtering arm, and bid the hosts obey."
  " If then thy will permit," (the monarch said,)
" To finish all due honours to the dead,
This, of thy grace, accord : to thee are known   830
The fears of Ilion, clos'd within her town ;
And at what distance from our walls aspire
The hills of Ide, and forests for the fire.
Nine days to vent our sorrows I request,
The tenth shall see the funeral and the feast ;   835
The next, to raise his monument be given ;
The twelfth we war, if war be doom'd by heaven ! "
  " This thy request," (replied the chief,) "enjoy :
Till then, our arms suspend the fall of Troy."
  Then gave his hand at parting, to prevent   840
The old man's fears, and turn'd within the tent ;
Where fair Briseïs, bright in blooming charms,
Expects her hero with desiring arms.
But in the porch the king and herald rest,
Sad dreams of care yet wandering in their breast.   845
  Now gods and men the gifts of sleep partake ;
Industrious Hermes only was awake,
The king's return revolving in his mind,
To pass the ramparts, and the watch to blind.
The power descending hover'd o'er his head,   850
And, " Sleep'st thou, father ? " (thus the vision said :)

  L. & C.

" Now dost thou sleep, when Hector is restor'd?
Nor fear the Grecian foes, or Grecian lord?
Thy presence here should stern Atrides see,
Thy still-surviving sons may sue for thee ;   855
May offer all thy treasures yet contain,
To spare thy age ; and offer all in vain."
    Wak'd with the word, the trembling sire arose,
And rais'd his friend : the god before him goes :
He joins the mules, directs them with his hand,   860
And moves in silence through the hostile land.
    When now to Xanthus' yellow stream they drove,
(Xanthus, immortal progeny of Jove,)
The wingèd deity forsook their view,
And in a moment to Olympus flew.   865
    Now shed Aurora round her saffron ray,
Sprung through the gates of light, and gave the day.
Charged with their mournful load to Ilion go
The sage and king, majestically slow.
Cassandra first beholds, from Ilion's spire   870
The sad procession of her hoary sire ;
Then, as the pensive pomp advanced more near,
(Her breathless brother stretch'd upon the bier,)
A shower of tears o'erflows her beauteous eyes,
Alarming thus all Ilion with her cries :   875
    " Turn here your steps, and here your eyes employ,
Ye wretched daughters, and ye sons of Troy !
If e'er ye rush'd in crowds, with vast delight,
To hail your hero glorious from the fight ;
Now meet him dead, and let your sorrows flow !   880
Your common triumph, and your common woe."
    In thronging crowds they issue to the plains,

Nor man, nor woman, in the walls remains:
In every face the self-same grief is shewn,
And Troy sends forth one universal groan. 885
At Scæa's gates, they meet the mourning wain,
Hang on the wheels, and grovel round the slain.
The wife and mother, frantic with despair,
Kiss his pale cheek, and rend their scatter'd hair;
Thus wildly wailing, at the gates they lay; 890
And there had sigh'd and sorrow'd out the day;
But godlike Priam from the chariot rose;
"Forbear," (he cried) "this violence of woes;
First to the palace let the car proceed,
Then pour your boundless sorrows o'er the dead." 895
    The waves of people at his word divide;
Slow rolls the chariot through the following tide:
E'en to the palace the sad pomp they wait:
They weep, and place him on the bed of state.
A melancholy choir attend around, 900
With plaintive sighs and music's solemn sound:
Alternately they sing, alternate flow
Th' obedient tears, melodious in their woe;
While deeper sorrows groan from each full heart,
And nature speaks at every pause of art. 905
    First to the corse the weeping consort flew;
Around his neck her milk-white arms she threw:
And, "Oh my Hector! oh my lord!" she cries,
"Snatch'd in thy bloom from these desiring eyes!
Thou to the dismal realms for ever gone! 910
And I abandon'd, desolate, alone!
An only son, once comfort of our pains,
Sad product now of hapless love, remains!

Never to manly age that son shall rise,
Or with increasing graces glad my eyes ;   915
For Ilion now (her great defender slain)
Shall sink a smoking ruin on the plain.
Who now protects her wives with guardian care?
Who saves her infants from the rage of war?
Now hostile fleets must waft those infants o'er   920
(Those wives must wait them) to a foreign shore !
Thou too, my son ! to barbarous climes shalt go,
The sad companion of thy mother's woe ;
Driven hence a slave before the victor's sword,
Condemn'd to toil for some inhuman lord :   925
Or else some Greek, whose father press'd the plain,
Or son, or brother, by great Hector slain,
In Hector's blood his vengeance shall enjoy,
And hurl thee headlong from the towers of Troy.
For thy stern father never spar'd a foe :   930
Thence all these tears, and all this scene of woe !
Thence, many evils his sad parents bore,
His parents many, but his consort more.
Why gav'st thou not to me thy dying hand?
And why receiv'd not I thy last command?   935
Some word thou would'st have spoke, which, sadly dear,
My soul might keep, or utter with a tear ;
Which never, never could be lost in air,
Fix'd in my heart, and oft repeated there ! "

    Thus to her weeping maids she makes her moan ;   940
Her weeping handmaids echo groan for groan.
    The mournful mother next sustains her part :
" O thou, the best, the dearest to my heart !
Of all my race thou most by heaven approv'd,

And by th' immortals ev'n in death belov'd !   945
While all my other sons in barbarous bands
Achilles bound, and sold to foreign lands,
This felt no chains, but went, a glorious ghost,
Free, and a hero, to the Stygian coast.
Sentenced, 'tis true, by his inhuman doom,   950
Thy noble corse was dragg'd around the tomb ;
(The tomb of him thy warlike arm had slain ;)
Ungenerous insult, impotent and vain !
Yet glow'st thou fresh with every living grace,
No mark of pain, or violence of face ;   955
Rosy and fair ! as Phœbus' silver bow
Dismiss'd thee gently to the shades below ! "
     Thus spoke the dame, and melted into tears.
Sad Helen next in pomp of grief appears :
Fast from the shining sluices of her eyes   960
Fall the round crystal drops, while thus she cries :
" Ah, dearest friend ! in whom the gods had join'd
The mildest manners with the bravest mind !
Now twice ten years (unhappy years) are o'er
Since Paris brought me to the Trojan shore ;   965
(Oh, had I perish'd, ere that form divine
Seduced this soft, this easy heart of mine !)
Yet was it ne'er my fate from thee to find
A deed ungentle, or a word unkind :
When others curs'd the authoress of their woe,   970
Thy pity check'd my sorrows in their flow :
If some proud brother eyed me with disdain,
Or scornful sister with her sweeping train,
Thy gentle accents soften'd all my pain.
For thee I mourn ; and mourn myself in thee,   975

The wretched source of all this misery !
The fate I caus'd, for ever I bemoan ;
Sad Helen has no friend, now thou art gone !
Through Troy's wide streets abandon'd shall I roam,
In Troy deserted, as abhorr'd at home ! "   980
　　So spoke the fair, with sorrow-streaming eye :
Distressful beauty melts each stander-by ;
On all around th' infectious sorrow grows ;
But Priam check'd the torrent as it rose :
" Perform, ye Trojans ! what the rites require,   985
And fell the forests for a funeral pyre !
Twelve days nor foes nor secret ambush dread ;
Achilles grants these honours to the dead."
　　He spoke ; and at his word the Trojan train
Their mules and oxen harness to the wain,   990
Pour through the gates, and, fell'd from Ida's crown,
Roll back the gather'd forests to the town.
These toils continue nine succeeding days,
And high in air a sylvan structure raise.
But when the tenth fair morn began to shine   995
Forth to the pile was borne the man divine,
And placed aloft : while all, with streaming eyes,
Beheld the flames and rolling smokes arise.
　　Soon as Aurora, daughter of the dawn,
With rosy lustre streak'd the dewy lawn,   1000
Again the mournful crowds surround the pyre,
And quench with wine the yet-remaining fire.
The snowy bones his friends and brothers place
(With tears collected) in a golden vase ;
The golden vase in purple palls they roll'd,   1005
Of softest texture, and inwrought with gold.

Last, o'er the urn the sacred earth they spread,
And rais'd the tomb, memorial of the dead.
(Strong guards and spies, till all the rites were done,
Watch'd from the rising to the setting sun.)   1010
All Troy then moves to Priam's court again,
A solemn, silent, melancholy train :
Assembled there, from pious toil they rest,
And sadly shar'd the last sepulchral feast.

    Such honours Ilion to her hero paid,   1015
And peaceful slept the mighty Hector's shade.

NOTES.

BOOK I.

Iliad : cf. Intr. p. xiii.

1. **wrath** : Intr. p. xii.   **Greece** : Intr. 4. d.   Cf. Arnold, on trans. H. p. 206.

2. **Goddess** : the muse. Cf. Milton, *P. L.* 1. 6, "Sing, Heavenly Muse"; *Odyssey*, 1. 1, "Tell me, O muse, of the man." Homer knows the Muses as daughters of Zeus, but he does not mention Mnemosyne as their mother, nor know them as "nine," except in the late passage, *Odyssey*, 24. 60.

3. **Pluto's gloomy reign** : Intr. p. xxv. (1) cf. Virg. *Æn.* 8. 244, *regna ... pallida. regnum*=kingdom. So "watery reign," l. 469; "Sirius' sultry reign;" "the reign of chaos and old night," *P. L.* 1. 543; "Ceres' golden reign " = fields of grain, etc., Gray.

4. **untimely** : the original has "hurled forward" or down, which Pope mistook for "hurled before their time."

5. **naked shore** : cf. 1. 472; 22. 125; 24. 499. Cf. "Sea-beaten rocks and naked shores | Could yield them no retreat." Cowper, *Bird's Nest.*

8. An "Alexandrine" line; cf. Intr. 6. c.

9. **Declare, O Muse** : Pope is following not Homer but Virgil *Æn.* 1. 8. *Musa mihi causas memora.* Cf. Intr. 1. b.

10. **offended power** : again Virgil, *quo numine læso.*

11. **Latona's son** : Apollo, whose shafts sent pestilence.

12. **mountains of the dead** : cf. l. 320; the hyberbole is un-Homeric.

13. **The king of men** : Homer says the son of Atreus, *i.e.* Agamemnon. Cf. Arnold, 207; "Milton says : —

' O for that warning voice, which he, who saw
The Apocalypse, heard cry in heaven aloud.'

. . . Homer would have said 'O for that warning voice which *John*
heard,' — and if it had suited him to say that John also saw the
Apocalypse, he would have given us that in another sentence."

13. **reverend priest**: in H. Chryses the priest.

14. Cf. Intr. 4. b.

17. **stands**: cf. Intr. 5. b.

18. **awful ensigns**: "a chaplet of wool, his symbol as priest of
Apollo, which as a suppliant he does not wear, but carries on his
staff" (sceptre 20). The "laurel," 20, is added by Pope after
Dryden, 1. 22.

22. **brother-kings**: Menelaus and Agamemnon.

26. **Safe to the pleasures**: added by Pope. So "if mercy
fail," 29.

28. **Chryseïs**: the captive daughter; cf. l. 16.

32. **"the fair"**: eighteenth-century "poetical slang," like
"fairest of her sex" and "brightest of the female kind." Cf. Intr.
p. xxiii.

35. **Hence on thy life**: so Dryden, 1. 45.

36. **what the king detains**: *i.e.* the girl whom I, the king,
detain.

40. Cf. l. 509.

41–42. In H. simply "till old age come upon her."

44. Antithesis not in Homer.

45. Argos generally means the Peloponnesus in Homer. Agamemnon was king of Mycenæ, not of the city Argos.

49. **anguish of a father**: decorative addition.

52. **The god who darts**: Homer does not explicitly identify
Apollo with the sun god. Cf. 55–56.

53. **Smintheus**: probably "destroyer of mice," from *sminthos*,
a mouse. Andrew Lang once amused himself by arguing that
Apollo was originally an animal god — a mouse totem.

54. **Cilla**: a town of the Troad. Tenedos, an island off the coast
in sight of Troy and the camp. Chrysa, a town of the Troad.

55. **source of light**: so Dryden, who explicitly says "sun."

56. **gilds**: "gild is a perfect ear-mark of eighteenth-century descriptive verse ; the shore is gilded, and so are groves, clouds," etc. — BEERS, *English Romanticism*, p. 58.

57-60. **If e'er**, etc.: the usual formula of Homeric and primitive prayer, reminding the god of past services and asking for a return. — **with wreaths**, etc.: in H. " roofed "; the fane was perhaps only a sylvan roof over a rude image. There are few temples in Homer. Cf. 6. 371 sqq.

61. **power**: cf. l. 10 ; Intr. p. xxv.

62. **Olympus**: mountain of Thessaly, mythic abode of the gods. The mountain towering into the clouds and the heavens themselves are not always clearly distinguished. In the *Odyssey* Olympus is rather " heaven " than the mere mountain. Cf. Jebb, p. 52.

63-68. Lessing in his *Laocoon*, XIII, quotes this passage to illustrate the superiority of poetry over painting in the description of life and action. " I not only see him descend, I hear him," etc.

65. **a sudden night**: in H. "and he descended like night." This and l. 644, " like the mist," are the only similes in the first book of the *Iliad* — both short.

67. **twang'd his deadly bow**: Cowper strives not very successfully to reproduce the suiting of the sound to the sense in the original, " dread sounding bounding on the silver bow."

68. **feathered fates**: from Dryden, 1. 74 ; cf. Intr. 4. d. So in Windsor Forest, " the clam'rous lapwings feel the leaden death " = bullets.

71. Nine is a conventional poetic round number in H. Cf. 6. 214-215 ; 24. 768.

74. **Juno**: Hera, wife of Zeus, partisan of the Greeks. Intr. p. viii.

75. **council**: the agora or general assembly of freemen foreshadowing our " lower house," as the Boulé or council of chiefs was the germ of senates and upper houses, while the commander-in-chief Agamemnon, with ill-defined powers, represents the king, president, or chief executive. Cf. Jebb, p. 49. — **Grecian train**: so Trojan train, female train, attendant train, ethereal train, hostile train, pious train, menial train, starry train, a train in tears, etc.

82. **remains of war**: Virgil's *reliquias Danaum, Æn.* I. 30. "The people which were left of the sword," Jeremiah 31. 2.

83. **prophet,** etc.; the original distinguishes: (1) soothsayer, who would accompany the army; (2) priest, attached to a particular shrine; (3) professional interpreter of dreams, mentioned only here.

85. **wasteful**: destructive; cf. l. 596 ; 6. 119.

86. Cf. Milton, *P. L.,* " For God is also in sleep and dreams advise."

88. **hecatombs** : offering of hundred oxen; then any offering.

89. **heaven** : Intr. 4. d. — **atoned** : *i.e.* at-one-ed, propitiated. Cf. Shaks. *Ant. and Cleop.* 2. 2 : " the present need | Speaks to atone you."

95. **Uprising slow** : Intr. 2. d.

96. Intr. 4. d.

107. **To whom Pelides** : Homer always introduces a speech by a whole line, and never omits the verb of saying. Intr. 5. e. — **Pelides** : son of Peleus, *i.e.* Achilles.

108. **and speak without control** : from Dryden, 129.

109. Cf. 52. n.

112. **vital air** : so Dryden, 131; Intr. I. b. *Rape of the Lock,* 4. 137. " While my nostrils draw the vital air."

116. **king of kings** : " Agamemnon," which is not fine enough for Pope.

119–120. **pest . . . priest** : Intr. 6. a.

126. Intr. 4. b.

128. **shining throne** : is not in Homer. The next ten lines are freely but vigorously rendered.

143. **Clytæmnestra** : wife of Agamemnon, mother of Orestes and Iphigenia.

144. **blooming beauties** : Intr. 4. a. and 1. d ; 24. 842. Dryden, I. 169, " in beauty's bloom."

145. **let her sail** : for sake of rhyme ; in H. " I am ready to give her back."

151. **the fair** : Intr. p. xxiii.

156 and 160. Cf. Intr. 4. b.

175. **or . . . or**: *i.e.* either . . . or, as often.

182. **plough the watery plains**: in H. "launch a ship on the great sea." The metaphor "plough," etc., is not in Homer, but Virgil has it, *Æn.* 2. 780. Cf. Intr. 4. c.

184. **laboring oars**: a Latinism frequent in Dryden's *Virgil.*

185. **sable**: Pope rarely deigns to use "black."

187. **Creta's king**: Idomeneus. So Dryden, I. 219.

194. **"armed with insolence"**: in H. "clothed in shamelessness."

195–196. **joined . . . mind**: Intr. 6. a.

198. **ambush**: cf. 299 n.

200–206: Pope fails in this picturesque passage. Cf. Intr. p. xxv. In H. " not by reason of the Trojan spearmen came I hither to fight, for they have not wronged me: never did they harry mine oxen nor my horses, nor ever waste my harvest in deep-soiled Phthia, the nurse of men; seeing there lieth between us long space of shadowy mountain and resounding sea." Chapman has: "hills enow, and far resounding seas, | Pour out their shades and deeps between." Cf. further Scott, *Lay of Last Minstrel*, 4. 6: " I had him long at high despite; | He drove my cows last Fastness night."

204. **native reign**: Cf. Milton, *P. L.* 2. 76, " native seat "; infra l. 335 and 6. 541.

208. In H. "to win vengeance, for Menelaus and thee." So in Achilles's great speech in the ninth book he asks: " But why must the Argives make war on the Trojans? Why hath Atreides gathered his host and led them hither? is it not for lovely-haired Helen's sake? Do then the sons of Atreus alone of mortal men love their wives? "

215–216. This clever conceit is Pope's. Cf. Intr. 3. a.

222. **Thessalia**: in H. " to Phthia," a district of what was later Thessaly, a word unknown to H.

225. This speech is rendered freely but vigorously with many un-Homeric antitheses and rhetorical touches.

239. **Myrmidons**: the subjects of Peleus and Achilles, according to legend, born of ants on the island of Ægina. Dryden actually renders, " and there thy ant-born Myrmidons command." From this

passage of Pope Myrmidons in English suggests "henchmen," "hire-lings," etc.

246. **Briseïs**=daughter of Briseus, the only name used for her by Homer. Achilles had slain her husband and three brothers and made her a "captive fair" at the sack of Lyrnessus. In the nineteenth book, when Agamemnon restores her, she utters a pathetic lament over the body of Patroclus, whom she finds slain on her return. Landor says playfully of Achilles: "Never night or day could be his | Dignity hurt by dear Briseis."

250. **kings are subject**, etc.: Pope is thinking not of Homer, but of Horace, *Odes*, 3. 1. 5; Intr. 3. c.

262. *I.e.* Hera or Juno.

264. **and by the golden hair**: a favorite scene with poets. Cf. Keats, *Hyperion*. "She would have ta'en | Achilles by the hair and bent his neck; | Or with a finger stayed Ixion's wheel." Mrs. Brown-ing, *Sonnets from the Portuguese*, 1: "a mystic shape did move | Behind me and drew me backward by the hair." Swinburne, *Tiresias:* "Lo thy sure hour shall take thee by the hair." Ruskin, *Queen of the Air*, 37: "There is an exquisite tenderness in this lay-ing her hand upon his hair, for it is the talisman of his life, vowed to his own Thessalian river if he ever returned to its shore, and cast upon Patroclus's pile, so ordaining that there should be no return."

265. **to him alone confessed**: the gods in H. generally appear to one person only. Pope adds the cloud. "Confessed" is after Virgil and Dryden. Cf. 22. 14; Æn. 2. 591, *confessa deam*.

269. **Descends Minerva**: Intr. 5. c.

276. **To reason yield**: this touch, added by Pope, suggests that Athena is only an allegory of wisdom. Intr. 2. b. Leslie Stephen, *Pope*, p. 68: "Pope does not feel that he is diverging from the spirit of the old mythology when he regards the gods, not as the spontaneous growth of the primitive imagination, but as deliberate contrivances intended to convey moral truth in allegorical fables." Ruskin, however, allegorizes without losing the poetry: "Through-out the *Iliad*, Athena is herself the will or menis of Achilles. If he is to be calmed, it is she who calms him; if angered, it is she who inflames him." Hegel says that in Homer the action of the gods

is so contrived as to seem to come at the same time from within
and from without.

291, 294. **blue-eyed maid . . . sacred senate**: cf. Intr. 4. a; I.
d; Dryden, 331, "senate of the gods."

297. In H. "Thou heavy with wine, thou with face of dog and
heart of deer."

299. **ambushed**: the ambush was looked upon as the supreme
test of courage. Cf. *Il.* 13. 276: "Nay, if now . . . all the best of us
were being chosen for an ambush — wherein the valour of men is
best discerned."

300. **horrid front**: Intr. 1. a. Milton, *P. L.* 1. 563: "a horrid
front | Of dreadful length and dazzling arms."

301. **fighting fields**: frequent in Chapman, Dryden, etc.

309. **sceptre**: the herald's staff, put in the hands of the speaker
to show that he "had the floor." Cf. Dryden's version of *Æn.* 12.
206: "Even as this royal sceptre (for he bore | A sceptre in his
hand) shall never more | Shoot out in branches, or renew the birth
| (An orphan now, cut from the mother earth | By the keen axe,
dishonoured of its hair, | And cased in brass, for Latian kings to
bear)." Pope parodies in *Rape of the Lock*, 4. 133: —

> " But by this lock, this sacred lock I swear,
> Which never more shall join its parted hair;
> Which never more its honors shall renew,
> Clipped from the lovely head where late it grew."

311. **as I from thee**: Intr. 3. a.

314-315. In H. "and now the sons of the Achaians that exercise
judgment bear it in their hands, even they that by Zeus' command
watch over the traditions." Cf. Jebb, p. 48.

320. Cf. 12. n.

328. Dryden adds, "and foam betwixt his gnashing grinders
churned."

330. **Pylian**: of Pylos on southwest coast of Peloponnēsus.

332. **Words sweet as honey**: Cf. Spenser, *Faery Queene*, 2. 3.
24: "And, when she spake, | Sweet words like dropping honey she
did shed."

I

341. **commit**: Intr. 1. a. — **stern debate**: l. 400; 22. 324. Dryden, 1. 10.

351 sqq. Very free.

353. **virtuous envy**: *i.e.* emulation, not in H.

354. **smit with love**: Virgil's *percussus amore, Georgics*, 2. 476; cf. Milton's "smit with the love of sacred song."

357. **Centaurs**: in H. wild beasts, "wild tribes of the mountain caves." Homer speaks of Cheiron justest of the Centaurs who educated Achilles, but he does not know the Centaurs as half-horse half man.

371. Added by Pope. Intr. 3. c.

373. Intr. 3. b.

383. Intr. 3. c.

385. **privilege**: *privilegium*, a law in favor of (or against) an individual.

388. **galling chain**: Intr. 4. c.

394. **secure**: Intr. 1. a., "Men may securely sin, but safely never."— **no more Achilles draws**, etc.: the clever epigram is not in H., though suggested by the speech quoted on line 208. Intr. 3. a.

401. Intr. 2. d.

407. Intr. 1. a. Milton, *P. L.* 1. 130: "That led the embattled Seraphim to war | Under thy conduct."

410. **expiate**: Intr. 1. a.

412. **pious train**: cf. 75. n.

417. **grateful**: added in imitation of Latin poets' use of *gratus*, acceptable. Cf. 6. 383; 22. 225. Dryden has "and clouds of savoury stench involve the sky!"

425. **ourself**: royal plural. Cf. Tennyson, *Princess*, "were you sick, ourself would tend upon you." In H., "I myself."

426. **act**: Intr. 1. a; 22. 108.

432. **Decent confusion**: Intr. 5. d. — **decent**: Intr. 1. a. Milton, "decent steps," "decent shoulders."

435. **sacred**: heralds were, of course, inviolable.

451. **sorrows**: tears. So Dryden often.

457. **That kindred deep**: the conceit is Pope's. Intr. 3. a.

461. **too severe a doom**: Milton has "doom severe," but Pope is thinking of Dryden's "Darius great and good by too severe a fate | Fallen." In H., "short-lived." For the thought of 460–464, cf. Arnold's *Early Death and Fame*.

469. **watery reign**: cf. l. 3.

478. **Thebè**: a town of Mysia.

483. **selected**: Intr. 1. a.

484 sqq. Cf. *supra*, 15 sqq. Homer repeats verbatim; Pope modifies a phrase here and there.

494. **peculiar**: own, special — a Latinism frequent in Dryden.

499. **points** (to); **derives**: traces as a river from its source.

507. Intr. 4. b.

509. Cf. *supra*, 40; Intr. 4. d.

514 sqq. This legend that the gods conspired to bind Zeus who was rescued by the hundred-handed monster Ægēon is a survival of an earlier religious age than Homer's.

518–519. *I.e.* Hera, Athena, and Poseidon. Cf. Intr. 4. a.

521. **omnipotence of heaven**: 2. b.

523. The fancy that some things are named differently in the language of the gods occurs about five times in Homer, and has become a familiar literary allusion. Its precise meaning is disputed. Ægeon may possibly = the man of the sea. Cf. Ægean Sea.

526–530. Pope here expands Homer, who is not fine enough for him.

534. **copious death**: Intr. 4. d.

537. **wide dominion of the dead**: added by Pope. Dryden (*Æneid*) has "waste dominion of the dead."

541. In H., simply "weeping"!

544–545. **short a space**: Intr. 5. a.

546. **careful**: full of care. So often. Cf. 22. 36; Spenser, *F. Q.*, "These be unquiet thoughts that careful minds invade."

544. **ethereal train**: cf. 643. Homer simply says, "Zeus and all the gods have gone to a banquet to the blameless swart-faces," but Pope's "nor disdain" softens for eighteenth-century readers the idea of the Deity so condescending. Intr. 2. b.

558. **genial rite**: Intr. p. xxv.

560. **mount**: mount to. So Milton and Tennyson use "arrive" for "arrive at."

566. Continuing 409. **rode**: *i.e.* his ship rode.

576. **awful dome**: Intr. 2. c.

581. **atoned**: *supra*, 89. — **desist to**: Intr. 1. a.

583. Added by Pope.

587. **salted cake**: unground barley grains, roasted and mixed with salt to be sprinkled on the victim. Pope is thinking of the *salsa mola* of the Latin poets. So Dryden.

603. **selected to**: Intr. 1. a.

604. **involved with art**: Latinism for "wrapped."

608. Intr. 1. a. So in Book XVI. "Arm, arm, Patroclus! Lo the blaze aspires."

609. **instruments**: in H., five-tined forks.

614. **rage of hunger was repressed**: Virgil's *amor compressus edendi*, *Æn.* 8. 184, which Dryden renders, "But when the rage of hunger was repressed."

616. **crowned**: *i.e.* filled to the brim. Virgil took it of crowning with flowers, *Æn.* 1. 724.

622 sqq. Chapman is rather pretty: All soundly on their cables slept, even till the night was worn | And when the Lady of the light, the rosy-fingered morn, | Rose from the hills, all fresh arose, and to the camp retired. | Apollo with a fore-right wind their swelling bark inspired. | The top-mast hoisted, milk-white sails on his round breast they put, | The mizzens strooted with the gale, the ship her course did cut! etc.

634. **navy**: freq. in Pope and Dryden for "ships."

636. **nor . . . nor**: so often for *neither . . . nor*.

640. **Twelve days**: *i.e.* from the scene that ends in 565.

643. **ethereal powers**: Milton, *P. L.* "Such I created all th' ethereal powers."

644. **like the mist**: cf. on l. 65.

645. **daughter of the sea**: Thetis.

649. **props the clouds**: cf. Thomson, *Autumn*, "Atlas, propping heaven as poets feign."

655. Intr. 4. b.

679. **sacred honours of our head**: Intr. p. xxv. So Dryden renders *Æn.* 10. 115: "The Thunderer said, | And shook the sacred honours of his head." Cf. *Eclogues*, 10. 24. This style culminated when vegetables were called "the honors of soups."

683–687. Cf. Milton, *P. L.* 2. 353, "And by an oath that shook Heaven's whole circumference, confirmed." For other parallels cf. Shorey on Horace, *Odes*, 3. 1. 8. Phidias said that his statue of Olympian Zeus was inspired by this passage.

685. **stamp of fate**, etc.: Dryden has "stamp of heaven and seal of fate."

690. **shining synod**: cf. 24. 130; Milton, *P. L.* 2. 391, "Synod of gods."

696. **silver-footed dame**: cf. song in Milton's *Comus*, "By Thetis' tinsel-slippered feet."

701. **In vain**: cf. on 22. 60.

705–711. Pope absurdly dignifies the wrangling of Zeus and Hera. Intr. 2. b. Cf. *infra*, 726 sqq., where Dryden's homely vigor errs as far the other way: "My household curse! my lawful plague! the spy | Of Jove's designs! his other squinting eye."

711. **close recesses**: 22. 566. Milton, *P. L.* 1. 795, "In close recess and secret conclave sat."

714. **Saturnius**: so Jupiter, as son of Saturn, is called by Latin poets.

719. **close consult**: cf. 6. 409. Milton has "close design," "close ambition," and "great consult." Dryden has "close contriver" here.

731. **What is, that ought to be**: lit. "if this is so, it is my pleasure;" but Pope makes Zeus speak the language of the *Essay on Man*, "whatever is, is right."

753. **double bowl**: formerly supposed to be a vessel with cup at either end. Probably such a two-handled cup as is shown in Schuchardt's *Schliemann*, p. 74.

760. **Once in your cause**, etc.: the original is somewhat softened by Pope. Intr. 2. b. Milton, *P. L.* 1. 740: "and how he fell | From heaven they fabled, thrown by angry Jove | Sheer o'er the crystal battlements; from morn | To noon he fell, from noon to

dewy eve, | A summer's day; and with the setting sun | Dropped from the zenith, like a falling star, | On Lemnos, the Ægean isle." Dryden has: "But with the setting sun | Pitched on my head at length, the Lemnian ground | Received my battered skull, the Sinthians healed my wound."

769. **nectared urn**: Dryden has a lovely line here, "The laughing nectar overlooked the lid."

770. **office**: Intr. 1. a; 24. 294. It was the office of Ganymede or Hebe. Cf. Dryden : "Such fits of laughter seized the guests to see | The limpy god so deft at his new ministry."

771. **unextinguished**: "Homeric laughter" is a familiar quotation. Cf. Mrs. Browning, *Aurora Leigh*, "and all true poets laugh unquenchably | Like Shakespeare and the gods."

772. **genial**: anything connected with feasting, pleasure, or love is "genial" in eighteenth century poetry. Cf. 1. 558; 6. 270; 24. 3.

775. **silver sound**: "Music with its silver sound." Shakspere, *Romeo and Juliet*, 4. 5. 136.

779. In H.: "where each one had his palace made with cunning device by famed Hephæstos." Cf. Intr. 4. a.

BOOK VI.

For synopsis of plot, cf. Intr. p. x.

4. **tide of combat**: Intr. 4. c.

5. **famed streams** : in H., Xanthus and Simois.

6. **run purple**: Milton, *P. L.* 1. 451, "ran purple to the sea."

10. **giant**: *i.e.* Acămas.

14. **swimming eyes**: not in H. cf. 22. 598; frequent in Dryden.

16. **Axўlus**.

17. **Arisba** : town in Troas.

19. **Fast by** : So Milton, *P. L.* 1. 12, "Fast by the oracle of God."

28. **Naiad**: fountain nymph. Cf. 531, mountain nymphs. Dryads and hamadryads are unknown to Homer.

32. Cf. 22. 538.

35–44. Astyălus, Pidȳtes, Aretāön, Ablērus, Elătus, Pedăsus, Eurypȳlus, Phylăcus, Leïtus, as the metre shows, — Nestor's son is Antilŏchus.

45–46. In H. " Menelaus took him alive."

54. **vengeful steel**: in H. " far-shadowing spear."

62. **steel well tempered**: lit. "smithied iron," *i.e.* hard to work as compared with the softer copper. Persuasive is added by Pope.

67. **impotent**: without self-control, 24. 53. Chapman renders "soft-heart."

70. **well merit**: Latinism, cf. 24. 263. Milton, *P. L.* "amply have merited of me."

74. **infants**: in H. "babes unborn." Intr. 2. a.

75. Intr. 3. b.

78. **To rigid justice**: in H. "advising fitly," a singular moral judgment to our feeling.

91. **Helĕnus**: brother of Hector, endowed with gift of prophecy.

93. **Æneas**: Intr. p. ix.

95. **Ye generous chiefs**: in H. "Oh Ænēas and Hector."

102. **hostile train**: 1. 75. n.

111. **power**: 1. 10. n.

114. **laboured o'er with gold**: cf. 24. 284, not in H. Virgil's *arte laboratæ vestes, Æn.* 1. 639.

115. **Before the goddess' knees**: on her knees. This is the only image explicitly mentioned in Homer. It would be of wood.

117. **atoned**: 1. 89. n.

119. **wasteful**: 1. 85.

136. *I.e.* the allies of the Trojans. Chapman, "far-called friends."

138. Intr. 3. a.

144. **The shield's large orb**, etc.: Cf. Milton, *P. L.* 1. 284: "his ponderous shield. . . . Behind him cast. The broad circumference | Hung on his shoulders like the moon."

147. **Now paused the battle**: so Pope tries to soften the naïveté of the long speeches that follow. Intr. 2. a.

154. **Where fame is reaped**: the metaphor not in H. Pope emphasizes the idea of fame throughout more than Homer.

158. **when Minerva fires**: added by Pope. In the fifth book

Athena abets Tydeides in wounding Ares and Aphrodite, and removes the cloud from his eyes that he may "know both god and man."

160. **no more**: Pope adds these words, perhaps to soften the contradiction which some critics find between Tydeides's caution here and his readiness to attack the gods in the fifth book.

161. **Lycurgus**: not, of course, the legislator of Sparta, but a mythical Thracian king represented as impiously opposing the new religion of Dionysus. Homer hardly alludes to Dionysus elsewhere, and the passage is thought an interpolation by some critics.

164. **Nyssa**: a mythical sacred mountain of Bacchus (Dionysus), of ill-defined situation.

165. **consecrated spears**: the so-called Thyrsus.

170. **blessed with endless ease**: Milton, *P. L.* 2. 868, "The gods who live at ease"; Tennyson; *Choric Song*, "On the hills like gods together," careless of mankind, *infra*, 24. 662.

175. **fruits of earth**: the gods owed their immortality to nectar and ambrosia.

177. **prodigal of breath**: Intr. 1. d. Cf. Horace, *Odes*, 1. 12. 37, *animæque magnæ prodigum*. "The spirit does but mean the breath," Tennyson.

181. **Like leaves**, etc.: often quoted and imitated in Greek and English literature. Bacchylides, Virgil, Dante, and Milton (*P. L.* 1. 302) use it of the dwellers in Hades.

184–186. Note the artificial repetition of "successive" and the antithesis of "these . . . those."

188. **spacious earth**: so "spacious air"; in H. "many men knew it."

189. **Argos**: 1. 45. n. — **utmost bound**: lit. in the recess of Argos, *i.e.* at the Corinthian gulf.

191. **Sisyphus**: in the *Odyssey* condemned for his guile to roll up hill a large stone that ever rolls back.

193. **Eph˘ré**: old name of Corinth. Pope's metre seems to require Ephȳré.

197. **Then mighty Prœtus**: Pope tells the story obscurely: Antēa, wife of Prœtus king of Tiryns (or Argos), loved Bellerophon,

an exile at her court. He spurned her advances, and she falsely
accused him to Prœtus, who shrank from killing Bellerophon, but
sent him to Lycia with a letter enjoining the Lycian king to engage
him in dangerous enterprises.

.202. **paths of fame**: like "devoted" and "relentless" youth
belong to Pope's rhetoric.

207. **his**: Bellerophon's.

208. **his**: Prœtus's.

209. **devoted**: cf. Milton, "to destruction sacred and devote."

210. **tablets sealed**: lit. "destructive tokens." There has been
endless debate whether this means sign, picture, syllabic, or alpha-
betic writing not elsewhere mentioned in H. Cf. Jebb, p. 112.

214. **Nine days**: 1. 71. n.

215. **orient gleamed**: Intr. 1. a. In H. "rosy-fingered dawn
appeared."

219. **Chimæra**: the only composite monster in the *Iliad*. H.
has no dragons, satyrs, or mermaids. Homer does not mention the
winged horse Pegasus, which later fable assigned to Bellerophon,
and which the moderns have made the Muses' steed.

223, 225. **expire . . . pest**: Intr. 1. a.

225. **read the skies**: lit. "trusting in the signs of the gods." H.
has no astrology. Cf. 22. 610; 24. 674.

227. **Solymæan crew**: the Solymi, a Lycian tribe.

229. **Amazons**: only here and *Il.* 3. 189, "the Amazons a match
for men."

234. **breathless**: "the blameless Bellerophon slew them all."

236. **confessed**: 1. 265. n.

242. Homer names them: Isandros, Hippolŏchus, and Laodameia.

244. **Sarpēdon**: Intr. p. ix.

247. **Aleian**: means field of wandering. Milton, *P. L.* 7. 17:
"Return me to my native element: | Least from this flying steed
unrein'd, as once | Bellerophon, though from a lower clime, | Dis-
mounted, on the Aleian field I fall | Erroneous there to wander and
forlorn." Cf. also "Behind me lies the broad Aleian plain | The
loneliest plain that faces to the sky; | Across which groping with

increasing pain | I course forever for I cannot die." William Rufus Perkins, *Bellerophon*.

254. **honoured author**: Intr. 4. a.

269. **Our ancient seat**: in the style of an English country gentleman. In H. "in our halls."

270. **genial**: I. 772. n.

275. **pledge**: the goblet; cf. 24. 288.

276. **still adorns my board**: "I left it at home." Intr. 4. a.

277. **Tydeus**: son of Œneus and father of the speaker. — **Thebé's wall**: the expedition of the seven against (Bœotian) Thebes, in which Tydeus took part, to restore to the throne the elder son of Œdipus, Polyneices, expelled by his younger brother Eteŏcles.

283. **harvest**: the metaphor is Pope's.

290. **Brave Glaucus**, etc.: a curious example of Pope's "softening" of the original. Intr. 2. a. H. says naively, "then Zeus took away his wits from Glaucus who," etc. Old Chapman, too, "alters this only of all Homer's original."

293. **nine oxen**: coined money is unknown to H. The Latin *pecunia* is derived from *pecus*, cattle. A tripod was worth perhaps 12 oxen, a female slave 4-20. — **vulgar**: frequent Latinism for cheap, common, 360; 22. 207.

296. **Meantime**: continuing 146.

297. **Scæan gate**: (in H. gates) and the oak tree (not beech) often mentioned. The "consecrated shades" not in H., perhaps suggested by the sacred laurel tree in *Æn*. 7. 60. 304-307. Cf. Virgil, *Æn*. 2. 503. In the original this is one of the chief texts for our knowledge of the Homeric palace, for which see Jebb, pp. 57-58. The "stately courts," "arched columns," and "marble structures" are added for dignity by Pope. Intr. 2. c.

312. **unseen of**: 22. 355.

315. Intr. 4. a.

316. **strict**: Intr. I. a.

322. **Bacchus**: so-called metonymy by which the god is put for his gifts. So Ceres = bread. Homer does not use "Bacchus" or "Dionysus" so, but he uses Hephæstus for fire.

326. **generous bowl**: not in H., but like "flowing bowl" frequent in Pope and Dryden.

330. Intr. 3. b. In H. simply "Bring me no honey-hearted wine, my lady mother, lest thou cripple me of my courage."

335. **Ill fits it me**: Cf. Dryden's version of Virgil, *Æn*. 2. 717: "In me 'tis impious holy things to bear, | Red as I am from slaughter, new from war."

362. **Sidon**: one form of the legend related that Paris and Helen touched at Egypt and Sidon on the way to Troy. Homer does not mention Tyre.

369. **majestically slow**: Intr. 2. d ; 24. 869.

371. **Palladian dome**: the temple of Pallas Athene on the Acropolis; but Pope wishes the reader to think of the "Palladian domes" of the great Italian architect Palladio.

372. Antēnor, Theāno.

382. **So**: *i.e.* if thou dost grant our prayer.

383. **grateful**: 1. 417. n.

391. **architects**: "builders."

393. **pompous structure**: Intr. 2. c.

399. **brother-chief**: Paris. — **useless arms**: the sneer is added by Pope.

409. **close resentment**: 1. 677, 711, 719.

411. Intr. 3. a.

417. Phrygian is used by the Greek dramatists and Latin poets as a synonym of Trojan. Not so in H. — **glories end**: cf. 573.

422. **thy brother**: Intr. 5. c.

427. Intr. 3. c.

428. **contain**: Intr. 1. a.

431. **lowly grace**: not in H.

432-433. In H. "My brother, even mine that am a dog, mischievous and abominable." Intr. 2. a.

434-439. Cf. Tennyson, *Dream of Fair Women* (Helen speaks): "Whereto the other with a downward brow: 'I would the white, cold heavy-plunging foam, Whirl'd by the wind, had roll'd me deep below, Then when I left my home.'" — "Golden sun," "fatal infant," and "fowls of air," are Pope's embroidery.

438. whelming tide: Milton, *Lycidas*, " Where thou, perhaps, under the whelming tide."

441. Paris of those ills the worst: the conceit is Pope's.

454. where glory calls: so in Pope and Dryden, "where honour calls," "where danger calls."

463. dearer part: cf. 624.

466. second joy: not in H. Hector was the first.

468-471. expanded from " stood upon the tower, weeping and wailing."

470. explore: Intr. I. a.

472-473. In H. simply, " And when Hector found not his noble wife within ! "

475. asked what way she bent: Pope abbreviates in indirect discourse what Homer gives in the direct form; the passage 477-487, also both in its omissions and additions, is a characteristic example of Pope's method.

480. " steepy tower ": from Dryden's version.

488. This parting of Hector and Andromache is one of the most beautiful passages in all literature. Pope's translation, his method once granted, is excellent; far better than Chapman's. The passage has been translated by Dryden, Mrs. Browning, and many others.

492. joyful fair: Intr. p. xxiii.

499. fair as the new-born star: in old Hobbes's version this runs : " And like a star upon her bosom lay, | His beautiful and shining golden head." Cf. Tennyson, *Princess*, " At her left a child, | In shining draperies, headed like a star."

503. Dryden renders, "From his great father who defends the wall."

504-505. In. H. " So now he smiled and gazed at his boy silently ! "

506. His beauteous princess : in H. *Andromache*.

519-520. In H. " But it were better for me to go down to the grave if I lose thee."

524. Achilles boasts in the ninth book that he sacked twelve cities by sea and eleven by land. Intr. p. x.

529. decent: I. 432. n.

536. **fat herds**: Pope does not try to render Homer's "kine of trailing gait" or "leg-plaiters" as George Eliot calls them.

539. **the queen**: "who was queen."

541. **native plain**: 1. 204. n.

543. **Diana's bow**: "Artemis, who showers her shafts," was the bringer of sudden death to women.

546–547. **Alas! my parents**: not in H. Pope thinks this antithetic repetition of 544–545 strengthens the thought. So Dryden, "O kill not all my kindred o'er again."

551. **fig-trees**: cf. 22. 193.

555. **Vengeful Spartan**: Menelaus. Intr. 4. a.

570–573. **Yet come it will**, etc. : these lines are repeated from Agamemnon's angry prediction of the punishment that awaits Trojan perjury, *Iliad*, 4. 163. Homer repeats them verbatim; Pope adapts them to the context : "The day shall come, that great avenging day, | When Troy's proud glories in the dust shall lay (sic), | When Priam's powers and Priam's self shall fall, | And one prodigious ruin cover all."

The historian Polybius relates that Scipio Africanus recited these lines with tears as he watched the burning of Carthage and reflected that the turn of Rome too must come.

580. **In Argive looms**: in H. simply "to weave the loom at another's bidding." The clever touch "our battles to design" is Pope's, suggested by Dryden's "gracing with Trojan fights a Grecian loom." "Woes of which so large a part was thine" was suggested by Virgil, *Æn.* 2. 6.

583. **Hyperïa**: or rather Hypereia, a fountain perhaps in Thessaly.

584. Dryden has "while groaning 'neath this labouring life."

599. Dryden has "and Hector hastened to relieve his boy."

600. **glittering terrors**: Intr. 4. d.

604–605. **O thou!** etc. : in H. "Zeus and ye other gods."

609. Intr. 3. a.

617. **pleasing burden**: "his child."

620–622. In H. "smiling tearfully." "I confess I doubt the Homeric genuineness of δακρυόεν γελάσασα. It seems to me much

more like a prettiness of Bion or Moschus." Coleridge, *Table Talk.*
Cf. "So sweetly gleamed her eyes behind her tears, | Like sun-
light on the plain behind a shower." Tennyson, *Merlin and
Vivien.*

624. **my soul's far better part**: added by Pope, who repeats
the phrase elsewhere. In Dryden's version of *Æn.* 4. 492, Dido
addresses her sister : " Witness, ye gods, and thou my better part ! "
Ovid has *parte meliore mei* of his soul and fame; and Macbeth in
Shakspere speaks of "my better part of man."

629. **hard condition**: Dryden also uses the phrase. Cf. Shakspere, *Hen. V.* 4. 1. 250, "O hard condition! twin-born with
greatness."

634-635. Lit. "war shall be the concern of men," a familiar
quotation in Greek literature.

645. **soft infection**: cf. 24. 644; 24. 983.

647. Pope abbreviates in this antithesis three simple lines of H.

652-659. Dryden thus renders Virgil's imitation of this simile
(*Æn.* 11. 492) : —

> " Freed from his keepers, thus with broken reins
> The wanton courser prances o'er the plains;
> Or in the pride of youth o'erleaps the mounds,
> And snuffs the females in forbidden grounds;
> Or seeks his watering in the well-known flood,
> To quench his thirst and cool his fiery blood;
> He swims luxuriant in the liquid plain,
> And o'er his shoulder flows his waving mane;
> He neighs, he snorts, he bears his head on high,
> Before his ample chest the frothy waters fly."

665. **stay**: 6. 457; 22. 307.

667. **in blood, and now in arms**: the conceit is Pope's.

672. **weeps blood**: Intr. 4. c.

678-679. "when we have chased out of Troy-land the well-greaved
Achæans."

679. **Greece indignant**: Intr. 1. b.

BOOK XXII.

Jebb, *Homer*, p. 32., selects this book for analysis. We recognize in it, he says, four general traits as preëminently Homeric: "(1) The outlines of character are made distinct in deed, in dialogue, and in audible thought. (2) The divine and human agencies are interfused. (3) Each crisis of the narrative is marked by a powerful simile from nature. (4) The fiercest scenes of war are brought into relief against profoundly touching pictures of domestic love and sorrow."

For events between Books VI and XXII cf. Intr. p. xi.

1. **panic fear**: "He had also the power of starting terrors, especially such as were vain and superstitious, whence they came to be called *panic* terrors." Bacon, *Fable of Pan*. Panic and Pan are not in H.

3. **briny drops**: Intr. 4. a.

4. **drown in bowls**: Intr. 4. c.

6. Lit. "setting shields to shoulders," perhaps a rudimentary form of the Latin *testudo*, for which see Cæsar, B. G. 2. 6. 2, in any good edition.

7. **embodied powers**: stately periphrasis. So even "cranes embodied," 3, 7. — Lines 8, 10, 11, added by Pope.

14. **confessed**: 1. 265. n. At the end of Book XXI Apollo in the guise of Agēnor lures Achilles to pursue him and so give the fleeing Trojans a respite.

18. **latent**: 24. 529.

21. **bestowed**: 24. 793.

30. **To cheat a mortal**, etc.: the original which Pope softens was censured as impious by Plato: "verily I would punish thee if I had the power." Intr. 2. a.

33. **victor of the prize**: cf. 24. 357, "victor of thy fears." Dryden has "victor of his vows."

36. **careful**: 1. 546.

39. **Orion's dog**: Orion, the great hunter, is seen in Hades by Odysseus. The constellation Orion, with the Pleiads, the Hyades, and the Wain, is depicted on Achilles's shield. The "dog" is Sirius

(not named in H.). It shines in the nightly sky only in the winter and spring. In the late summer dog days of which Homer speaks it appears just before dawn. Pope adds the "thick gloom," etc., and interprets late summer as autumn, a season unknown to Homer. — **weighs**: apparently suggested by the Latin *gravis* — (sickly, oppressive) *autumnus, gravi anni tempore*, etc., or possibly weighs = balances in the scale of the constellation Libra. "Year" for season of year is a common Latinism in eighteenth-century poetry.

40. **exerts**: Latinism, *exsero*, thrust out. So Dryden, *Æn.* "So from the seas exerts his radiant head | The star, by whom the lights of heaven are led."

41. **Terrific glory**: Intr. 5. d. For the simile, cf. Tennyson, *Princess*, "And as the fiery Sirius alters hue, | And bickers into red and emerald, shone | Their morions washed with morning as they came."

45–48. **obtests . . . expects**: Intr. 1. a.

51. Intr. 5. a.

54. **fury of the plain**: like "terror of the plain," frequent periphrasis in Pope and Dryden.

55. Intr. 5. f.

60. **Valiant in vain**: not in H. Virgil uses *frustra, nequicquam* of virtue, valor, or happiness that do not avail in the end, and this pathetic "in vain" is a note of eighteenth-century poetry. Cf. Gray, *Eton College*, "Ah, fields beloved in vain," etc.

63. **explore**: Intr. 1. a.

65. Lycāon's death at the hands of Achilles is described in one of the finest passages of the *Iliad*, 21. 34–135.

66–67. Cf. 6. 58–61.

68. **grandsire**: Altes, king of the Lelĕges. Cf. 21. 85, "Old Altes' daughter and Lelegia's heir." The wealth is a sort of dowry which he gave with his daughter, one of Priam's wives.

71. **Stygian coast**: (from Styx, the river of hell), like "Stygian shore," "Stygian flood," etc., Latinizing paraphrase common to Milton, Dryden, and Pope. Homer knows the Styx as the river by which the gods swear.

79. **Neglect**: Latinism *nec-lego*, not heed.

87. Intr. 3. a.

93. **relic** : Intr. 1. a.

95-107. Pope softens and sophisticates the affecting natural touches of the original here.

98–99. Intr. 3. c.

101. **honest** : honorable, cf. 364.

108. **acting** : 1. 426.

111. **sorrows** : tears.

112. **zone** : belt, not in H., where she pulls open the front of her dress (by loosening the brooch on one shoulder).

113. **falling** : transitive.

115. **words of age** : Intr. 4. d.

121. **but heaven avert it** : not in H.   Like Latin *absit omen*.

130. **the** : generalizing "the" of similes.   Virgil, *Æn.* 2. 411, imitates this simile, and Pope is thinking of Virgil and Dryden as much as of Homer.   "Brake" is from Dryden; "turgid," not in H., is Virgil's *tumidum*.

134. **collected ire** : a Latinism: Lucret. 1. 723, *colligere iras*.

137. Cf. Milton, *P. L.* 6. 113.   "And thus his own undaunted mind explores."

139. **Ungenerous** : ignoble.   "Generous" is of noble birth and breeding.

140. Lit. " Polydămas will be first to bring reproach against me." In. 18. 254. Polydamas had advised retreat after Achilles's return to the war.

149. Intr. 3. a.

. 162. **produce** : *pro-ducere;* cf. 24. 332.   Shakspere, *Julius Cæsar* 3. 1. 228. "Produce his body to the market place." 166; Intr. 6. c.

167. **We greet not here** : Pope spoils this lovely idyllic vision in the midst of the horrors of war, " no time is it now to dally with him from oak-tree or from rock, like youth with maiden, as youth and maiden hold dalliance one with another." — **conversing** : (with) cf. 210.

173. **Thus pondering** : *i.e.* while Hector thus pondered.

175. **Pelian** : "his great paternal spear, | Ponderous and huge

K

which not a Greek could rear ; | From Pelion's cloudy top an ash entire. | Old Chiron fell'd, and shaped it for his sire ; | A spear which stern Achilles only wields, | The death of heroes and the dread of fields." *Il.* 19. 389–392. (Pope).

175. **in his better hand :** "brandishing from his right shoulder."

177. **beamy splendours :** of the celestial armor made by Hephæstus at the prayer of Thetis in the eighteenth book.

179–180. **unusual terrors** and **struck by some god :** are added by Pope, perhaps to soften Hector's flight for modern readers. Cf. Lang, *Homer and the Epic*, p. 210. "In a saga, or a *chanson de geste*, in an Arthurian romance, in a Border ballad, in whatever poem or tale answers in our northern literature, however feebly, to Homer, this flight round the wall of Troy would be an absolute impossibility. . . . Can we fancy Skarphedin, or Gunnar, or Grettir, or Olaf Howard's son flying from one enemy?"

184. **liquid skies :** so Dryden, "cleave the liquid sky." Gray, *Spring*, "float amid the liquid noon."

193. **fig-trees :** 6. 551.

194. **smoke along :** not in H. Cf. Dryden, *Æn.* 7. 909, "Proud of his steeds he smokes along the field."

195. **Scamander's double source :** two springs answering fairly to Homer's description have been found on Mt. Ida twenty miles away from "Troy."

201. **marble cistern :** "washing-troughs, fair troughs of stone." Intr. 2. c.

204. **washed their fair garments :** so Odysseus finds the "Princess" Nausicaa and her maidens washing at the river.

207. **no vulgar :** 6. 293. n.

210. **contended** (for) : cf. 167.

216. Intr. 3. a. — **raised :** excited; Latin, *erectus*.

224. Cf. 24, 44, 45.

225. **grateful :** 1. 417. n.

228. **Fate :** Intr. 4. d.

240. **I give the fates their way :** not in H., and more in the manner of Seneca or Lucan.

242. **Tritonia :** Trito-born, unexplained epithet of Athena.

244. **beagle**: a small dog for hunting hares; in H. simply "dog."

247. **vapour**, etc.: *i.e.* the scent.

248. **certain**: *certus*, unerring.

256. In H. "but he (Achilles) ever ran on the city-side."

257. **As men in slumbers**: this, the earliest simile from dreams, is imitated by Virgil, *Æn.* 12. 908, where Æneas pursues Turnus; in Dryden's version: "And as when heavy sleep has closed the sight, | The sickly fancy labours in the night; | We seem to run, and destitute of force, | Our sinking limbs forsake us in the course," etc. Cf. Tennyson, *Vision of Sin*, "But as in dreams, I could not."

263–266. The original is obscure.   Pope paraphrases.

266. **nerves**: sinews.   Intr. 1. a.

267–269. **great Achilles . . . signed**: Aristotle in his *Poetics*, speaking of the difference between epic and drama, says that this scene would be ridiculous on the stage.

271. **golden balances**: this image is borrowed by Virgil, and by Milton, *P. L.* 4 *in fine*. In Milton the lighter scale of the weaker combatant mounts.

276. Intr. 6 c.

280. Intr. 4. d.

282. **drunk with renown**: Intr. 4. c.   Cf. Kipling, *Recessional*, "Drunk with sight of power."

285. **he**: Apollo.

291. **martial dame**: Intr. 4. a.

294. **voice belied**: feigning voice.

317. **Enough**, etc.: the turn of the phrase is Latin.   Cf. Virgil, *Æn.* 2. 642, *satis vidimus exscidia*, etc.

322. **suspend**: 24. 839. — "**day**" is often used for "battle" or "issue."

346. **'Tis Pallas, Pallas**: *i.e.* Pallas Athena; a curious example of Pope's preoccupation with Virgil. In the *Æneid* Turnus has slain Pallas, a youth beloved by Æneas. When Turnus falls before Æneas, Æneas exclaims, in Dryden's version, "'Tis Pallas, Pallas gives this deadly blow."

347. This fancy is Pope's. Homer says, "Now in one hour shalt thou pay back for all," etc.

350-352. **meditated . . . innocent**: Intr. 1. a.

355. **unseen of**: cf. 6. 312.

361. Intr. 3. b.

362. **false terrors**: "unreal." Cf. Horace, *Epistles*, 2. 1. 212, *falsis terroribus implet.* — **sink**: transitive.

364: **dishonest**: *supra*, 101; 24. 66.

368. Intr. 6. c.

370. **heavenly**: cf. 177. n.

371. **resulting**: *resulto*, rebound. Intr. 1. a. 386-388. In H. "At least let me not die without a struggle or ingloriously, but in some great deed of arms whereof men yet to be born shall hear." Cf. Tennyson, *Two Voices:* "To perish, wept for, honoured, known | And like a warrior overthrown; | Whose eyes are dim with glorious tears | When, soiled with noble dust, he hears | His country's war-song thrill his ears."

399. **Hesper**: cf. Milton, *P. L.* 4: "Hesperus that led | The starry host rode brightest."

412. **thy**: the shift to second person is Pope's. Homer naively says, "*so that* he (Hector) might speak words of answer to his foe."

417. Added by Pope. Cf. Dryden's version of Virgil, *Æn.* 10. 94. "Then was your time to fear the Trojan fate!"

418. Intr. 3. a.

421. **he**: Patroclus.

427. **prevalence of prayer**: "I pray thee by thy knees."

438. **no — to the dogs**: the clever, softening turn is Pope's. Intr. 3. a; 2. a; 24. 262.

451. **Phœbus and Paris**: they slew Achilles in "the things after Homer." Cf. Lang, *Helen of Troy*, 5. 42, "But now, their leader slain, the Trojans fled, | And fierce Achilles drove them in his hate, | Avenging still his dear Patroclus dead, | Nor knew the hour with his own fate was great, | Nor trembled, standing in the Scæan gate, | Where ancient prophecy foretold his fall; | Then suddenly there sped the bolt of fate, | And smote Achilles by the Ilian wall.'

455–458. Matthew Arnold's imitation is truer to the spirit of Homer than Pope : —

> "Till now all strength was ebb'd and from his limbs
> Unwillingly the spirit fled away,
> Regretting the warm mansion which it left,
> And youth and bloom and this delightful world."
> —SOHRAB AND RUSTUM.

460. **unheard**: in H. simply "him even dead Achilles addressed."

467. **some, ignobler**: the moralizing is added by Pope. But cf. 24. 66–69, where the sentiment is attributed to the gods that it is ignoble to insult the dead.

469. **How changed that Hector**: in H. "far easier to handle is Hector now"; but Pope is thinking of Virgil's *quantum mutatus ab illo Hectore, Æn.* 2. 274.

485 sqq. "dear image" (cf. 24. 6), "vital spirit" and "flames" belong to Pope's rhetoric.

493. Intr. 2. d.

494. Cf. Shakspere, *Troilus and Cressida*, 5. 9 : —

> "On, Myrmidons, and cry you all amain,
> *Achilles hath the mighty Hector slain.*"

496. **Unworthy**: cf. 467. n.

497. **nervous**: 266. n.

502. **his**: Hector's.

519. **spires**: Intr. 2. c.

527. **impotence**: 6. 67. n.

528. **in dust**: "in the mire or manure of the courtyard." Intr. 2. a.

536. **He has a father, too**: cf. 24. 599. n.

547. Intr. 4. a.

555. **Patient of**: Intr. 1. a. So Dryden, "Patient of human hands and earthly steel."

566. Intr. 2. c. — **close recesses**: 1. 711. n.

580–581. **desert . . . heart**: Intr. 6. a.

589. **jaws of fate** : Intr. 4. c.

598. **swimming eyes** : 6. 14.

600–602. On headdress of Homeric women, cf. Jebb, p. 64.

608. In H. her first word is " Hector — woe is me."

610. **one star** : 6. 225. n. ; 24. 674.

611. **Hippoplacia** : 6. 495.

636. **The kindest**, etc. : Pope abstractly paraphrases Homer's concrete expression, " and one of them that pity him holdeth his cup a little to his mouth and moisteneth his lips, but his palate he moisteneth not."

638. **Frugal compassion** : Intr. 5. d.

643. **Astyanax** : the mother suddenly shifts from the general thought to her fears for her own son.

659. **Useless to thee** : the primitive thought here which Pope misses is that the burning of the garments will not profit Hector's shade because he will not be burned on the pyre with them.

BOOK XXIV.

1. **games** : the funeral games in honor of Patroclus, described in the twenty-third book.

3. **genial** : 1. 772.

6. **dear image** : 22. 485.

7. Added by Pope.

8. **gifts of sleep** : a phrase used by H. ; not here, but 7. 482; 9. 714. So Milton, "thy gift of sleep." — **all-composing** : in H. "that conquereth all." Cf. *Dunciad*, 4. 627, "the all-composing hour."

10. Intr. 4. c.

29. **skies** : Intr. 4. d.

37. *I.e.* Juno. Intr. 4. a.

38–41. Intr. p. viii.

44–45. Cf. 22. 224.

53. **impotence** : 6. 67.

57. The Greek poets often moralize that the sense of shame is

the greatest good, and yet, in the form of shamefacedness or false modesty, a great evil.

59. **repugnant**: *re-pugnans*. Intr. 1. a.

63. Matthew Arnold's favorite line, "For an enduring soul have the Destinies given to men."

66. **dishonest**: 22, 364.

68–69. Cf. **22. 467. n.**

73. **Then hear**, etc. : that is, "listen to Apollo."

78–83. Cf. Intr. p. viii.

96. **azure queen**: *i.e.* Thetis, goddess of the blue sea. Intr. 4. a.

101–102. In H. "leaped into the black sea!"

103. **Samos**: *i.e.* Samothrace; the *Iliad* does not know Samos.

106. **profound**: a noun; cf. *inane profundum*, and Milton's "palpable *obscure.*"

107–108. Pope omits the picturesque Homeric particulars. "And she sped to the bottom like a weight of lead that mounted on horn of a field-ox goeth down bearing death to ravenous fishes." The lead was the "sinker," and the bit of horn perhaps protected the line. Homer rarely alludes to fishing, and the Homeric man eats fish only under stress of famine. — **fallacious** : in that it cheats the fishes, a Latin conceit not in H.

112. Intr. 4. a.

113. **revolving**: Lat. *revolvens*, brooding over, or, possibly, "reading the book of." Not in H.

115. **goddess of the painted bow**: so Dryden, *Æn.* "goddess of the various bow," "various Iris," etc. Homer does not, like Virgil, *Æn.* 4. 701, think of Iris messenger of the gods as the rainbow.

124. **majestically sad**: Intr. 2. d. Dryden, *Æn.* "majestically sad he sits in state."

125. **world of waters**: not in H.

130. **shining synod**: cf. 1. 690.

138. **maternal sorrows**: Intr. 5. d.

146. **this glory**: *i.e.* of self-conquest. Intr. 3. b.

168–172. **indulge . . . relics**: Intr. 1. a.

184. **decent**: 1. 432; 6. 529.

194–195. Intr. 3. b.

195. **down her bow**: not in H.; cf. 115. n.

202. **ashes**: 22. 528. n.

204. **vaulted dome**: Intr. 2. c.

233–234. In H. simply "Lady, from Zeus hath an Olympian messenger come to me."

246. **overthrown**: not in H. Cf. *Hamlet*, 3. 1, "O what a noble mind is here o'erthrown!"

249. **wander o'er**: not in H. Apparently let thy eyes (or lips?) wander o'er.

261. **in his dearest blood**: lit. "whose inmost vitals (liver) I were fain to fasten and feed upon." Cf. Intr. 2. a; 22. 437. Cf. Beatrice in *Much Ado*, "I could eat his heart in the market place."

263. **merit thus**: Intr. 1. a; 6. 70.

264. **expired**: *ex-spiro*, breathe out.

273. **present goddess**: Latinism, *præsens deus*, Horace, *Odes*, 3. 5. 2. "A present deity! they shout around, | A present deity! the vaulted roofs rebound." Dryden, *Alexander's Feast*.

275 sqq. Intr. 5. f.

277–279. In H. "let Achilles slay me with all speed, when once I have taken in my arms my son," etc.

284. **stiff with gold**: not in H. Virgil, *Æn*. 11. 22, *vestes auro . . . rigentes.* Cf. 6. 114.

286. **talent**: in H. a small weight; later about $1200.

288. **pledge**: *pignus*, 6. 275.

290. **one last look**: not in H. Intr. 3. a.

294. **office**: service, *officium*, 1. 770. Tennyson, *Morte d'Arthur*: "And thou the latest left of all my knights, | In whom should meet the offices of all." ·

307. **Oh, send me gods**: cf. 6. 518.

309. **feebly**: added by Pope.

311. **erring**: going astray, added by Pope.

317. **Inglorious sons**, etc.: "I always was particularly struck with that passage in Homer, where he makes Priam's grief for the loss of Hector break out into anger against his attendants and sons, and could never read it without weeping for the distress of that

unfortunate old prince." Pope, in Spence's *Anecdotes.* "When
Priam had his whole thoughts employed on the body of his Hector,
he repels with indignation, and drives from him with a thousand
reproaches, his surviving sons, who with an officious piety crowded
about him to offer their assistance. A good critick (there is no
better than Mr. Fox) would say that this is a master-stroke, and
marks a deep understanding of nature in the father of poetry. He
would despise a Zoilus, who would conclude from this passage that
Homer meant to represent this man of affliction as hating, or being
indifferent and cold in his affections to the poor relicks of his house,
or that he preferred a dead carcase to his living children." Burke,
Appeal from the New to the Old Whigs.

322. **Troilus**: in H. only here, but an important name in literature from Virgil, *Æn.* 1. 474, and the mediæval story of " Troilus
and Cressida," in Boccaccio, Chaucer, Lydgate, and Shakspere's
play.

329. "Harness the mule car!"

331-332. In H. "fearing their father's voice." Intr. 2. a, or
3. b. — **produce**: 22. 162. n.

335. **Box was the yoke**, etc.: the disputed technicalities of the
original, which Pope loosely paraphrases, do not concern the literary student of Pope's *Iliad.*

357. **Victor of**: 22. 33. n.; the antithesis "thy . . . mine" is
Pope's.

358. **Heaven or thy soul**: in H. simply "since thy heart
speedeth thee." Cf. Virgil, *Æn.* 9. 184 (Dryden). "Or do the
gods inspire | This warmth, or make we gods of our desire?" In
what follows, Pope "heightens the style" by such phrases as
"desolated realms," "sovereign of the plumy race" = eagle, "yon
ethereal space," "who so good as Jove?"

364. **tower**: Milton has "towering eagles." *P. L.* 5.

388 sqq. In H. "sent forth an eagle, surest omen of winged
birds, the dusky hunter, called of men the Black Eagle " (percnos !).

393. **stooping dexter**: term of augury for Homer's "speeding
on the right hand."

411. **Hermes**: Pope here employs the Greek name (not Mer-

cury).   Hermes sometimes takes the place of Iris as messenger of
the gods in H.   Later he became the patron god of heralds.

415. **prevent**: Intr. 1. a.

417. **golden pinions binds**, etc.: Cf. Virgil, *Æn.* 4. 350
(Dryden).   "Hermes *obeys*.   *With golden pinions binds* | His
flying feet, and mounts the western winds; | And whether o'er the
seas or earth he flies, | With rapid force they bear him down the
skies."

418. **incumbent**: Milton, *P. L.* 1. 225, "Then with expanded
wings he steers his flight | Aloft, *incumbent on the dusky air.*"

421. **wand**: the so-called Caduceus.   Cf. Tennyson, *Demeter
and Persephone*, "the serpent-wanded power" = Hermes.

424. **Hellespont's resounding sea**: periphrasis for "Hellespont."

425–426. In H. "in semblance as a young man that is a prince,
with the new down on his chin, as when the youth of men is come-
liest."   Cf. Milton's Uriel as a "stripling cherub," *P. L.* 3.

426–427. In H. simply "darkness was come down over the
earth."   Intr. 4. c.

429. **What time**: Milton, *P. L.* 1. 36, "what time his pride," etc.

430–431. In H. simply "beyond the great barrow of Ilus . . .
at the river."   Pope makes of it a picturesque landscape in the
style of Claude Lorrain or Salvator Rosa.

448: **sealed**: Intr. 4. c.

457. **lines**: lineaments.

465. In H. "All this old sire hast thou verily spoken aright;"
but Pope is unwilling to let the imputation of falsehood rest on a
god.   Intr. 2. b.

477. **tempt**: Intr. 1. a.

481. **I saw him when**: Book 15. 718; 16. 123.

484. **enjoyed the fire**: added by Pope.

485. **Myrmidonian**: 1. 239. n.

491. **watch**: *i.e.* as sentinel.   In Homer simply, "and now I am
come from the ships to the plain."

502. Intr. 4. a.

515. **or all**: *i.e.* or else not merely some but all.

522. **in exalted power**: *i.e.* when alive and in power.

523–524. In H. "Therefore they have remembered it for him, albeit his portion is death." Intr. 3. b. c.

529. **latent**: 22. 18. H. does not think it necessary to remind us that Hermes is disguised.

530–536. Intr. 3. b. In H. "I were afraid and shamed at heart to defraud him, lest some evil come to pass on me hereafter." Pope makes explicit the antithesis of the two motives, shame and fear.

544. **not their own**: a favorite turn of eighteenth-century diction, ultimately derived from the Latin of Virgil's grafted trees that wonder at *non sua poma*, "apples not their own." *Georgics*, 2. 82. Cf. *Rape of Lock*, 1. 148, "And Betty's praised for labours not her own."

547. **virtue of his wand**: magic potency, specific quality. Cf. Milton's "Virtuous ring and glass," and Shakspere's *Merchant of Venice*, 5. 1, "If you had known the virtue of the ring." In H. virtue is manly virtue, *i.e.* courage.

549. **massy**: Intr. 1. c.

552. **tent**: obviously a tent only in the general sense of soldier's dwelling.

563. **and thus revealed**: Intr. 5. e.

568. Lit. "It were cause of wrath that an immortal god should thus show favor openly unto mortals."

578. Intr. 2. d.

592. **just gains some frontier**: in H. "to the house of some rich man and wonder possesseth them that look on him."

599. **Think of that father's age**: a delicate psychological touch, for in 22. 536 the first thought that occurs to Priam when he sees Achilles trailing Hector from his car is "he has a father, too."

603. Intr. 3. a.

615. **pledge**: in eighteenth-century diction = child, in imitation of the Latin poets' use of *pignus*.

617. Intr. 3. a.

630. **Thus forced to kneel**, etc.: in H. "and have braved what none other man on earth hath braved before, to stretch forth my

hand toward the face of the slayer of my sons." But it has been generally taken in the sense " kiss the hands of the slayer." "Till Priam did what no man born hath done, | Who dared to pass among the Argive bands, | And clasp'd the knees of him that slew his son | And kissed his awful homicidal hands." Lang, *Helen of Troy*, 5. 30.

644–646. These lines are perhaps the most ludicrous travesty of a pathetic original in all Pope.

663. **Two urns**: a bit of moral philosophy in the form of a myth. There is mixed good and evil, and unmixed evil in the world, but no unmixed good.

669. **meagre**: *i.e.* emaciating; in H. "ox-hunger," ravenous hunger.

671. **sincere**: *sincerus*, unalloyed; sometimes fancifully explained as honey without wax, *sine cera*.

674. **stars**: 6. 225. n.; 22. 610.

675. **a realm**: Phthia. — **a goddess**: Thetis.

681. **him**: Achilles.

682. **his**: Peleus's.

683. **Thou too, old man**: Arnold, *On Translation of Homer*, pp. 295–296. "The most essentially grand and characteristic things of Homer are such things as . . . ' nay and thou, too, old man, in times past wert, as we hear, happy.' In the original this line, for mingled pathos and dignity, is perhaps without a rival even in Homer."

689. **from his bitter urn**: added by Pope. It is not in Homer's simple manner to follow up an image in this way.

698. **on the bare beach**: in H. "at the huts."

712. **not thy own**: 544.

717. In H. "lest I leave not even thee in peace."

742. **touch the ghosts**: "touch" is a reminiscence of *tangere*, used in the same way by Latin poets. Cf. "If aught of things that here befall | Touch a spirit among things divine." Tennyson. *Duke of Wellington.*

752. **paints**: a note of eighteenth-century diction.

753. **But now**, etc. : "But now bethink we us of supper. For even fair-haired Niobe bethought her of meat."

762. **Cynthia**: Artemis, Diana from Mt. Cynthus on Delos, her native isle.

778. Intr. 3. a.

779. Intr. 6. c.

785. "And many tears shall be his due."

796. Cf. 1. 614. n.

800–801. Pope develops the antithesis. Cf. Intr. 4. b.

805. **dew of sleep**: not in H. Intr. 4. c. Shakspere has "golden dew of sleep," *Richard III.* 4. 1; Milton, "dewy sleep," *P. L.* 9; Shelley, *Adonais VII.;* Virgil, *Æn.* 3. 511, *sopor irrigat artus;* Persius, 5. 55, *irriguo somno.*

809. **my only food**, etc.: Intr. 3. a.

821. **prevent**: Intr. 1. a.

832. **aspire**: Intr. 1. a.

839. **suspend the fall**: in H. simply, "I will hold back the battle."

842. **blooming charms**: 1. 144.

869. **majestically slow**: Intr. 4. d; 6. 369.

900–905. Note the un-Homeric artificiality of these lines.

907. **weeping consort**: "white-armed Andromache."

930. **For thy stern father**: this misses the pathos of the original "for not gentle was thy father in the grievous fray," *i.e.* as we knew him gentle at home. Cf. the "Lullaby" in the *Golden Treasury,* p. 36: "Although a lion in the field, | A lamb in town thou shalt him find."

931. **Thence all these tears**, etc.: *i.e.* "therefore the people lament him," because he was "a lion in the field." Pope seems to miss the meaning.

938. **never, never**: Intr. 5. a.

942. **mother**: Hecuba. —**sustains her part**: "led the loud lament."

959. **pomp of grief**: Dryden has "pomp of woe."

960. **shining sluices**: Milton, *P. L.* 5. 133: "Two other precious drops that ready stood, | Each in their crystal sluice" = two tears. This lament of Helen is one of the most touching things in the *Iliad.* Pope is not very successful with it. Readers of "Tom

Brown " will remember the scene in which " little Arthur " breaks down over it. Cf. Lang, *Helen of Troy*, 4. 9 : "and in the court of Ilios were two | Kind hearts still eager Helen to defend, | And help and comfort in all need to lend : | The gentle Hector with soft speech and mild, | And the old king that ever was her friend, | And loved her as a father doth his child."

992. **gathered forests** : "great store of wood."

994. **sylvan structure** : "lofty pyre."

1015. **such honors** : "Thus held they the funeral for Hector, tamer of horses."

ADVERTISEMENTS

An Introduction to Robert Browning.

By HIRAM CORSON, LL.D.,
Professor of English Literature in Cornell University.

THE purpose of this volume is to afford aid and guidance to the study of Robert Browning's Poetry. As this is the most complexly subjective of all English poetry, it is, for this reason alone, the most difficult. The poet's favorite art form, the dramatic, or rather psychologic, monologue, which is quite original with himself, presents certain structural difficulties, but difficulties which, with an increased familiarity, grow less and less. The exposition of its constitution and skillful management, presented in the Introduction, and the Arguments given to the several poems included in the volume, will, it is hoped, reduce, if not altogether remove, the difficulties of this kind. In the same section of the Introduction certain peculiarities of the poet's diction are presented and illustrated.

It is believed that the notes to the poems will be found to cover all points and features of the texts which require explanation and elucidation. At any rate, no real difficulties have been wittingly passed by.

The following Table of Contents will indicate the plan of the work : —

Cloth. 348 pages. $1.00.

D. C. HEATH & CO., Publishers

BOSTON   **NEW YORK**   **CHICAGO**

An Introduction to Shakespeare.

By HIRAM CORSON, LL.D.,
Professor of English Literature in Cornell University.

THIS work indicates to the student lines of Shakespearean thought which will serve to introduce him to the study of the Plays as plays. The general introductory chapter is followed by chapters on: The Shakespeare-Bacon Controversy, — The Authenticity of the First Folio, —The Chronology of the Plays, — Shakespeare's Verse, — The Latin and Anglo-Saxon Elements of Shakespeare's English. The larger portion of the book is devoted to commentaries and critical chapters upon Romeo and Juliet, King John, Much Ado about Nothing, Hamlet, Macbeth, and Antony and Cleopatra. These aim to present the points of view demanded for a proper appreciation of Shakespeare's general attitude toward things, and his resultant dramatic art, rather than the textual study of the plays. The book is also accompanied by examination, questions.

This work is a scholarly and suggestive addition to Shakespeare criticism, especially suited to students' use, by reason of the author's long experience as a teacher, and also valuable to all lovers of Shakespeare, by reason of its independence of opinion, originality, and learning.

The Nation : Altogether, so excellent a volume of Shakespeare criticism has not been put forth by an American scholar in many a day. Teachers and students both may profit by it as a model of how to learn in this particular subject.

Cloth. 400 pages. $1.00.

D. C. HEATH & CO., Publishers

BOSTON   NEW YORK   CHICAGO

AN INTRODUCTION TO THE

Study of English Fiction.

By WILLIAM EDWARD SIMONDS, Ph.D.

Professor of English Literature, Knox College.

ENGLISH fiction is eminently worthy of the attention of the stu-dent of literature, and the history of its development is a sub-ject not unsuited to the methods of the class-room. The purpose of this volume is to provide material for a comparative study of our fiction in its successive epochs, and for an intelligent estimate of the characteristics and merits of our story-tellers in the various stages of their art. The book is inductive in plan. A brief historical outline is presented in five introductory chapters which bear the following titles: I. Old English Story Tellers. II. The Romance at the Court of Elizabeth. III. The Rise of the Novel. IV. The Per-fection of the Novel. V. Tendencies of To-day. VI. Books for Reference and Reading. These chapters are followed by twelve texts illustrative of the different periods described. These selections are: I. Beowulf. II. King Horn. III. Arcadia. IV. Forbonius and Prisceria (entire). V. Doron's Wooing. VI. Shepherds' Wives' Song. VII. Jack Wilton. VIII. Euphuism (from "A Margarite of America"). IX. Moll Flanders. X. Pamela. XI. Tom Jones. XII. Tristram Shandy.

F. J. Furnival, *The Shakespearian, London, England :* I'm glad you've written on fiction. It is the greatest power in literature now, and has been the least studied scientifically. You've done the right thing.

R. G. Moulton, *Professor of Literature in English, University of Chicago :* You are rendering a great service to literary education in recognizing fiction as a field for inductive treatment. The arrangement of the work will greatly increase its practical usefulness.

Cloth. 240 pages. 80 cents.

Briefer Edition. — Without illustrative selections.
Boards. 91 pages. 30 cents.

D. C. HEATH & CO., Publishers

BOSTON   **NEW YORK**   **CHICAGO**

Webster and Burke.

Edited by A. J. GEORGE, A.M.

Select Speeches of Daniel Webster.

WEBSTER'S name is unquestionably the greatest in American political literature; it is the only one that can stand comparison with Burke's. These selections represent him in the several distinct fields in which his genius manifested itself so powerfully,— before the Supreme Court, in the Senate, before a jury, on a great historic occasion, as a eulogist, and in a national election.

Cloth. 404 pages. 75 cts.

Burke's Speeches on the American War,
and Letter to the Sheriffs of Bristol.

THIS work is edited in the hope that, by furthering the study of the greatest political classic in the English language, it may also further that spirit which seeks to study history as revealed in literature, and literature as inspired by great historical events. In the preparation of the notes, the editor has confined himself to the historical setting and interpretation of the work.

Cloth. 254 pages. Introduction price, 50 cts.

Webster's First Bunker Hill Oration.

With preface, introduction, and notes.
Boards. 54 pages. Introduction price, 20 cts.

Burke's Speech on Conciliation with America.

With introduction and notes.

BOTH of the above selections are set for the college preparatory work, the examination upon which "presupposes a thorough study of subject-matter, form, and structure of the period, tendency and type of literature," which they represent.

Boards. 117 pages. Introduction price, 25 cts.

D. C. HEATH & CO., Publishers

BOSTON   **NEW YORK**   **CHICAGO**

Wordsworth.

Edited by A. J. GEORGE, A.M.

Wordsworth's Prelude.

An Autobiographical Poem.

THIS work is prepared as an introduction to the life and poetry of Wordsworth. The poet himself said, " My life is written in my works." The life of a man who did so much to make modern literature a moral and spiritual force cannot fail to be of interest to students of history and literature.

Cloth.   354 pages.   Introduction price, 75 cts.

Selections from Wordsworth.

THESE selections are chosen with a view to illustrate the growth of Wordsworth's *mind and art;* they comprise only such poems of each period as are considered the poet's best work.

The method of annotation used in the edition of the *Prelude,* has been followed here; a method which insists upon the study of *literature* as *literature,* and not as a field for the display of the technicalities of grammar, philology, and poetics.

Cloth.   452 pages.   Introduction price, 75 cts.

Wordsworth's Prefaces and Essays on Poetry.

IN these various essays we have the evolution of that poetic creed which has made Wordsworth rank among the great critics of the century.   Mr. George has collected and illustrated them by allusion to the principles of criticism which have prevailed from Aristotle to Matthew Arnold.

Cloth.   133 pages.   Introduction price, 50 cts.

D. C. HEATH & CO., Publishers

BOSTON   NEW YORK   CHICAGO

www.ingramcontent.com/pod-product-compliance
Lightning Source LLC
Chambersburg PA
CBHW031100280326
41928CB00049B/1176